BLUE ARC WEST

AN

ANTHOLOGY

OF CALIFORNIA

POETS

BLUE ARC WEST

AN

ANTHOLOGY

OF CALIFORNIA

POETS

TEBOT BACH • HUNTINGTON BEACH • CALIFORNIA • 2006

Editor: Paul Suntup
Assistant Editors: Dima Hilal, Mindy Nettifee

Design, layout, cover design: Melanie Matheson, Rolling Rhino Communications
Cover photography: Robert Lanphar

ISBN-13: 978-1-89367-021-1
ISBN-10: 1-89367-021-X
Library of Congress Control Number: 2006907381

Tebot Bach, Welsh for *little teapot*, is A Nonprofit Public Benefit Corporation which sponsors workshops, forums, lectures, and publications. Tebot Bach books are distributed by Small Press Distribution, Armadillo, Ingram, and Bernhard De Boer.

www.tebotbach.org

This anthology was made possible by a grant from **The San Diego Foundation Steven R. and Lera B. Smith Fund** at the recommendation of Steve and Lera Smith.

blue arc west

contents

BLUE ARC WEST

AN

ANTHOLOGY

OF CALIFORNIA

POETS

Neil Aitken
After Neruda

After Neruda,
you hear the sea in everything,
its great bell-like waves sounding
deep in your anxious sleep, moving invisibly
by your ears with each passing car.

Light takes on a strange quality,
like the once-familiar scent of women
you have known or the texture of old bus tokens,
worn smooth in pockets, no longer in currency.

Suddenly, everything is a woman.

The way a street lamp curves
at the edge of a dark street,
or an orchid blooms in an empty room
patient for destruction, beautiful as a white slip
floating in the wrecking ball's wake.

Suddenly you wish to make love
in a language you do not know,
or write prayers between the lines
of old dollar bills given to strangers.

You caress the backs of pews,
pray to unknown gods you have witnessed
from your window, their half-closed eyes
flashing in the distance, like lighthouses in a storm.

In the kitchen, you surround yourself
with apples, lemons, and a tomato.
Arranging them in silence, you can sense
her presence just beneath the skin.

When you hold the tomato to your ear
you can hear her breathing in ragged sighs,
like a ship heaving against the tide.
When you press it to your lips,
you can still taste the unwashed salt of sorrow.

Neil Aitken
Pomello

Wandering the Granville Market aisles
my mother pauses mid-stream,
between salmon and cheese,
her hands curl hesitantly around a pomello,
suddenly uncertain of how one chooses
outside of taste.

Was it by sound, texture, shape,
or scent?

Was it weight?
she wonders,
remembering limbs bent low
in late summer,
the grass full of fallen suns
blazing in a green sky
at her feet.

How it hefts in the hands?

She chooses, pays, leaves.

Later, she will remove its thick husk
with a sharp knife, sink teeth into its bitter flesh,
and be startled by a taste
she no longer knows.

William Archila
This is for Oscar

It always starts here,
over the chain-linked fence
        with crooked fingers

and leather shoes, running
across the railroad tracks,

        no sound but a gasp
for breath, our white shirts flipping
like flags, the cops in black behind.

Sometimes, it's you kneeling
at the corner of the liquor store, handcuffed,
        a baton blow
to your back, flopping
to the ground, a grunt
        of flesh and bone,
your golden tooth sobbing.

This is what I remember when I drive
through east L.A., the boys leaning
        against the wall, rising above trash
                cans and beer bottles,

baggy pants and black
shades, long white shirts
        with two clown faces
above the left breast: one laughing,
                the other crying.

        I think
we were fifteen
when we worked in the dark kitchen,
                the restaurant heat
                        of vegetables and spices,
bags of rice and boxed beer from China.

During breaks, you stood in the alley,
        your shirt over the shoulder
like a towel, whistling
at the girls strolling

their short skirts, exposing
        the lighter skin
                of their bodies.

Around midnight, after carrying
	the last crate of dishes, we untied
our wet aprons.

		I sat across from you
munching on loaves of bread, Italian sausages,
swigging on a bottle of wine,
your talk thick as honey-
			marijuana visions of North
			America: blonde girls and their bikinis,
			low riders at night, you in a zoot suit
				and Bruce Lee.

Fifteen years will pass
before I think of you again,
your deportation to a village
	between cane fields at dusk,

		your disappearance between the Eucharist
		and the clang of the bell
			early Sunday morning.

I'm a teacher now,
fingers full of chalk, papers piled around me.
	Sometimes, in the dark eyes
	of students, you appear,
		your white shirt and shiny shoes,

		your back slouched
		at the board, cracking the English grammar,

and it all starts again,
climbing over the fence, through east L.A.

On a street corner, a boy
flashes a hand sign.

Carol W. Bachofner
History

is always happening:

like last week
when

lit by a wooden match,
a thousand acres
of old trees burned.

Or yesterday
when people began

hoarding water
in glass jars like the ones
their grandmothers used
to conserve peaches, rhubarb.

Around your neck,
history too

in the soft pouch where
your umbilical cord
remains, saved evidence

that you once got along
perfectly
with your mother.

Loops of collapsed
vein and arteries testify,
flattened hard like amber:

your dna suspended
like a bee's wing or hind leg.

Terry Bat-Sonja
Against the Crystal

Damn these inner thighs,
which gave you such pleasure,
and thank God for my heart,
which beats despite it all.

Awakening to butter colored
sheets, and the citrine crystal
I slept on, so hot now, imprinted,
my essence smoked into
its transparency.

Heat falls away from unseen
precipice, coarse grass grows
wildly ignorant over your stone.

The sky has been overcast
for days. It's a shaded way
to go deeper, dip the quill,
and not evade.

More and more order in this
house creates only more room
to look, never finding that tongue
and eye dialogue we shared.

Something that no candles,
incense, or humming bird feathers,
such delicate portents can ever fully
assuage.

I cannot understand this delicate
dissolution, interrupted now by the cats
sealpoint paws, then finally, suddenly
by sleep, sleep against this gentle crystal,
where there is some reprieve.

Joan E. Bauer
On the Poetics of the Text

We will consider:
The shift from radically free
postmodern textuality to more traditional artistic form.

> *she abducted beauty   blue woman-child*
> *   abducted   the halo-moon*
> *   the strange embittered trees*

We will ask the questions—
Is the text playful?
Is it a semiotic artifact
tenable in the after-postmodern period?

> *green stem circling*
> *   clasping tendrils of desire*
> *beauty I have no right to hold*

Is it a construct only
or does it flow from the felt world?

> *beauty I hold regardless*
> *hummingbird I hear*
> *   your whirring in the silence*

Papers. The overlap of poetical/textual
linguistic semantic philosophical
gender/cultural

> *pollinate*
> *   she-fire   he-rain*
> *breathe*
> *   the orange exploding sky*

Richard Beban
Heroes

Before the company moved & took his
job with it, my father made pencils
shorter all day long. He carried home

stubs & we drew, never as well as he,
since my brother was five & I was only
three. One Saturday, Dad bought a bag of

nineteen-cent burgers & three dime shakes & we
picnicked there, a second-floor room of steel
desks, wooden swivel chairs & grime dark

windows like thin scrims softening piers, cargo
ships, & the riveted undergirders
holding the silver span that ended in

hated Oakland, home to the cross-bay Oaks,
rivals to our Seals, DiMaggio's
first team. Dad, head bent, clicked his ivory

slide rule & drew tiny numbers with his
longer pencils, while my brother & I
used #1 graphite stubs on the backs

of used graph paper to draw what we saw
outside: round canary sun, Jap Zeroes strafing
brave battleships through red blossoms of flak

in the fabled war that ended a month
before brother was born; black deuce coupes with
scarlet flamed hoods & fenders outrunning

Tyrannosaurs thanks to zig-zag speed lines
we drew behind each coupe. Sneaking looks at
Dad, I copied his posture, concentration,

except his tongue didn't droop absently
out the corner of his mouth. From then on,
we knew where our stubs came from, how special

Dad was that they trusted him to work
alone, on a weekend, in that room full
of important desks, with dinosaurs just

outside the windows. When the stubs stopped, I
stole pencils at Woolworth's, but never played
work with Dad again.

Marjorie Becker
Furrows in the Open Land

We were in the Hotel Guaraní bar,
Asunción and me glistening with heat.
Why all this "te quiero,
te quiero?" At least my village
novio opened me properly.
All this strut and tease,
strut and tease. Who taught you that
necessity? You said you had a girlfriend
in your own village,
but weekend after weekend
you borrowed your reliable country horse,
checked the fish pond my neighbors dug,
crawled into my room.

You were an outrage.
I think I hated you
for your every strength
the ways with a word
campesinos changed their predictable enough ways,
worked different tools,
made furrows in the open land,
that warm begging soil
lush after rain
waiting for anything.
Julio,
I knew those guys too
in the most Biblical sense,
but when you went to them,
stumbling out of my bed, life,
moistened your lips,
they re-furrowed.

That night you told me
you liked the cling of my blouse,
you made me wild with sorrow.
I didn't know, as we drank,
as I raged, as your hands worked my legs,
as the heat persisted, as though we, even you,
affect anything at all, I didn't know
I would remember you always and forever,
3 marriages later, 5 kids,
each one more adept at making cheese straws,
I would wait, and not at a distance.
We are fifty now and Julio, oh God,
you're better than you were. I don't just mean

you find me in Istanbul, Constantinople-that-was,
in Cuenca, in Byron, Georgia,
you find me as I work the world,
sharing what Paraguay taught me,
that there is only flesh, all is temporary,
you find my chest, heart, hands,
again, again, oh Julio,
dream a future for us,
a future.

Lory Bedikian
Night in Lebanon

The youngest boy, with his ulcer,
sleeps. His lower lip pulsates, a small fish
breathing. A bed of torn pillows, cradles four
of them, two brothers, two sisters —
curved, quiet on the living room floor.
Buzzing, the open window has its mouth full
of street lights, mosquitoes, those who stay
awake. Peeled paint on the ceiling, the door

sheds the skin it wore through
a drawn-out, twenty-year civil war.
The parents sleep in a room full of faith
hammered to the walls. Posing, a copper
cross, its inscription in Armenian asks
for blessings of God upon this home.
Through the mother's sleeping lips a prayer
slips, rises, drifts and hovers above the boy

who dreams: he's a grown man
spinning yarn around their home
until it's as thick as a bomb shell.
Then, cane in hand, walking through a cedar
grove, he drops his string of worry
beads into a well. Cracking a pumpkin
seed open with his teeth, he tastes
childhood in each closed casing.

In the morning, a thin scroll
of bread filled with tomato paste, oil, mint
will start the hurried day. But now, he sleeps
as he did the day he was born. Stillness
enters his lip, his mouth finally rests,
breathing as he will when he is older
than this war whose finger has carved a scar
in him, the size of an eye that will not close.

Keven Bellows
Losing It

Unsheathed, my mother's voice whirred
like the knife-thrower's weapon
toward the girl in the spotlight.
Anger set her edgewise to me.
The surface of the words thinned,
strained against the limits of love,
stung me into isolation
the color of glaciers.
Caught in a confusion of echoes—
barbs piercing the air—I waited
for the blindfold to be lifted.

When she died she left me her tools,
rusty blades still sharp enough
to separate me from my own children,
frozen tone pinning them at safety's edge
as they diminish across a divide,
widening with every word.

Laurel Ann Bogen
Safety Pin

Holds together the torn off,
the haunted slip straps,
and buttonless collars.
Utilitarian to the end,
it fits into itself with a click:
fastened,

reliable,
I think.
When we piece our wounded papers,
our overdue notices together,
it secures them.
Like you to me.

Laurel Ann Bogen
Sanctuary

I come to you, a penitent
arms full of lilies,
calla and stargazer,
these serene trumpets
and I, who took the word sin
and tasted it,
turned in on myself
like a many-chambered
mollusk, neither loaf
nor fish, truly
I say to you
I was consumed.

With stained vestments
I cloaked myself
in taffeta or lace.
A liturgy of magpies
screeching *mea culpas*
cut through me —
I stumbled
through corridors of stone.

I loved no breath
of children sleeping,
no starling's flight,
no touch, or mirrored face.
I loved no one.

What survives is ink and bone,
the only altar I come to
in the white hour.

Constant and still
you wait to welcome me, bitterroot,
the beloved, an inspiration,
my sanctuary, my host.

Deborah Edler Brown
Still Lives

The sorrow of shapes is not sorrow
but a longing for the wordless then,
the everything, the nothing
that a thing can hold.
Word is insufficient.
Even apple, shell, rock
fails them.

The red world of firm flesh is eternal and frail.
Bite into it and it reincarnates as
imagination, corpuscles,
red dreams of satin curtains,
the Santa Monica fires.

The rock is the grandchild
of the ground we stand on
and its little finger.
The heart breaks to see it alone,
prays it company, breathes easy
when it loves the shell.

We are meant to be alone
and yet we are not.
It is the paradox,
the split knowing
of creation.

The ceramic tower, blue-green vase,
mimics the sky, the trees below it.
It seems big but is fragile.
The pinky of the earth could make it dust.
It will not. They are cousins.
One lives in the expanse of dirt and sky.
One burned in the apple flame
after hands have squeezed and shaped it.
Still, it dominates the conversation.
The world is restful in its absence:

I must bite the universe in tender portions:
a small red world, a mollusk's home
which sings like a shofar when the wind goes through.
The silent shape of things calls.

Derrick Brown
A Short Song

the ultra sound photo sat on your lap
like a note you had to sit down to read
a war letter to a mother

an infinite grief
wrapped your shoulders in a black mink
the nauseousness left covert
snuck from the theater of your gut
and your new healthy feeling meant terrible news

like a lover with fists you will miss
if you could still be sick for 2 more months
you would

what do i say?

the option of a funeral
or leaving it at the hospital
a doctor voicing this with the importance of fries or soup

maybe the child was too amazing for earth
maybe God is an indian giver
maybe the angel of death is as fast as a bored policeman
and just as dangerous

now you are tested and expected to carry on
to begin again

the vacancy signs of motels made you weep

you are not a morgue
you are a factory of mudfights and beauty
and if the assembly line goes on strike
negotiate
and things will start running again

when the doctor told you a day before the funeral
that it was actually a girl, I know it hit you harder
the confusion. the name change. the small clothes abandoned
girls seem to deserve to die less

i watched your boys play on the cemetery trees
how i wanted us to join them

i noticed
at most funerals
the only room for an audience
is among the grass and graves
seated on plastic chairs with velvet covers
upon the sloganed tombstones of the departed flights

i wept
sitting on a man's grave with a long name
wondered, not about the huge way i sneezed
or kissed nervously, but if someday
a boy would
sit upon mine
and when his plastic chair rickets back
he might see my name
and notice that graves are things we walk upon
and must walk away from

if I could uninvent shoebox sized caskets
i would do this for you.

Linda Brown
Coyote Darshan*

1.

Last August I saw you as a dog
limping along a suburban road,
underfed, a mat of shaggy hair
centered midback on your rack of bones.
At my approach you fled into a driveway
pretending to be the family pet.
But I was circling the neighborhood
and came upon you again.
As I gazed into your eyes,
I saw you were no dog.

When you knew I'd guessed your secret,
you trotted sideways onto the street
nervously looking back. A lean season
for cats: your fur, gone. I wished
I had a dish of water, some raw hamburger
with me in the car. I followed you five blocks
like the second mourner in a funeral cortege.
Forgotten—all the cat owners frantic with loss.
A gold Mercedes turned the corner.
You leapt for the shelter of a bush.
Did you survive? I will always remember
that odd island of fur on your spine,
all that was left of your coat.

2.

The road ribboned up
into Joshua Tree National Monument.
Mica embedded in blacktop
glinted into my eyes.
Where the road flattened
among those million-year-old rocks
there you sat unmoving
in the exact center of the road.
I stopped to pay homage,
to look past your black nose tip
into your wild eyes.
The sun backlit your guard fur,
a healthy ruff with well-fed sheen.
You seemed tame.

Let me receive
your *darshan*. I want your calm.
I claim, as you have, this star-splashed highway,
this ancient tumble of boulders
this high desert stillness
as home.

* *Darshan* is the gaze of a holy being; to receive *darshan* is considered a blessing.

Mark Bruce
Elegy for a Goldfish

Larry was the middle one,
the goldfish who was not as big
as Harry, who stunted
Jerry's growth. The afterthought
in the tank, who often chased
the smaller and hid from
the larger. And yesterday
as I was cleaning the tank,
having put the three into a smaller bowl,
I noticed Larry on his side,
his oval mouth moving slowly. The other two
swam at the top of the bowl,
noses stuck into the water's edge
as if afraid to go near
the dying fish. I put them back
into the tank, and let Larry
lie on his side, alone
in the bottom of the small bowl.
I sat watch for him, waited
for his fins to stop moving;
he would gamely rise
a few inches every few minutes,
but the end finally came
and he drifted at last to the bottom
his black eyes unmoving.
I thought of saying a few words
to speed him on his way, but I knew
fish are agnostics, and thought
Larry would resent
my spiritual intrusion on what was,
after all, nothing more
than a small bulb's light
which flickers, then is dark.
I will give him to the soil
beneath a rose bush, allow him
the dignity of decay, of feeding
nutrients into the soft earth,
encouraging the bloom
of orange gold blossoms,
which nod in the current of the wind
a flash of gold in sunlight,
a flick of fin-shaped petal in rain.

Christopher Buckley
Dispatch from Santa Barbara, 2001

Mid-summer, July 4th in fact, but I'm not in town for the fireworks display from the breakwater. I'm here on errands, an emergency trip to the dentist, in and out before they crown East Beach, Ledbetter, and the harbor, packing in on the sand thick as grunion under a phosphorescent moon.

I have an hour before I have to be somewhere, and I stop in Alameda Park where my mother first brought me as a child. There was a pool of shade under some trees and no swans drifting a little lake, no roses, no hedges in the shape of a heart—precious little except the wood bandstand that even then was no longer in use. Little but that block of shade—Anacapa to Santa Barbara Street, Micheltorena to Sola—courtesy of Morton Bay Figs and Spanish palms, and the creamy, book-perfect, fair-weather clouds of the '50s going over the Figueroa range—since age 4, the clouds and trees carrying off my thoughts....

And today I think of Thomas Wolfe, the sad line anyone knows about home. He knew about time, the quick dusty path here below the clouds. Perhaps he knew what was coming with real estate on the California Coast, way back when everyone lived in bungalows....Now, making more money that I ever imagined, I am nonetheless dispossessed, can only afford to live an hour north in the wind and fog. I stand here, my feet on a sidewalk worn rough as beach sand, pavement I've walked off and on for 50 years, looking up to the blue or to the old clear stars, and it's hard to call it mine.

My work is 3 hours south of here, and so I'm driven in all senses, past what I love. This morning, I'm taking time off from the world to be in it, to turn back—in star time—an instant, to 50 years ago when my mother took me after a nap out to the free, green republic of the park, from our turquoise stucco apartment on Micheltorena. We had just moved here and no one had heard of Santa Barbara, no one cared it was here an hour-and-a-half above L.A., a sleeping arboretum even angels overlooked, where we had next to nothing, and everything, where father worked nights, and my mother and I ate fried bologna and tomato soup in the Formica kitchen in front of a GE plastic radio. I had this life beneath the cool plush oaks and I didn't know to ask for anything more.

The bandstand still standing...the small metal harp at the top, the cupboards for dwarfs all around underneath...the criss-cross walk corner to corner, the honorary wino in this black thrift store suit and white tennis shoes, smoking alone by the chained-off steps leading to the platform where I raced around in circles when I was 4...the 2 obligatory people passed out on the grass, newspapers over their faces, the early silent heavy air going by, slowly it seems...

Beneath the star pines and magnolias, the voluminous pittosporum, the 1 jacaranda pushing out for sun, the 5 paltry redwoods, the single eugenia grown exponentially beyond hedge size, older than me...I'm counting trees, so I keep it this time. And I want to name the St. Joseph's candle thrown out thick and twisted, to appeal to Our Lady of Sorrows with its washed-out pink walls and bell tower across the way, as if this, or any of these lost listings could help me reclaim or hold my home.

This park, this place, as full and spare as I remembered it at 4—no adornment but the leaves, the carved top of the picnic table, someone's initials sunk beneath the brown paint, from Catholic High up the street in 1954, the bare civic patched raked, and sprayed with a hose—part of the world that doesn't miss me, where, if I could, if I had more time, the simple wherewithal of dirt, I'd be here all my days, content as the trees for all the sky to see. As the acorn woodpecker laughing at God, and his good fortune, at the same sparrows and rogue pack of pigeons claiming the earth or whatever is left of it here alongside the 1 picnic table and the grass as they peck at the grains of light....I join them again today, holding on to everything the wind has left to offer....

Elena Karina Byrne
Paradise Mask

*It was a popular medieval belief that paradise, a land or island where everything was
beautiful and restful, and where death and decay were unknown, still existed somewhere
on earth. It was usually located far away to the east and in the 9th century maps it is shown
in China, and the fictitious letter of Prester John to the Emperor Emanuel Comnenus states
that it was within 3 days journey of his own territory—a "fact" that is corroborated by
Mandeville. The Herford map (13th century) shows it as a circular island near India.
—Brewer's Dictionary of Phrase & Fables*

For you are invisible
as an undiscovered island
and ready to rehearse for the end
which is a sickly sweet nothingness
whispered into everyone's ear, the fuchsia
elsewhere you long for, blue
at the end of the barometer, and
the lasting grace of green rising
around you, glittering.
It must be true.
Your heart still depends on it,

granting you this:
Paradise exists, the between-world
you want so badly, contagious
and proven by word of mouth, just
a smooth stepping stone-throw
away from here.
This is

the planted seed in your mind's black eye
or call of the wild at the lid of Pandora's box.
This is stopped time
cupped in the mouth of a calla lily, withdrawn
denizen's milk-dream from death, Nirvana's
underside, Cornucopia's compass
the size of Texas, and after that, the circle
you fall into
to save yourself from drowning
or from making the simple mistake that all else
will faithfully end
no further than here.

Mary Cahill
A Letter For V

There is a table by the window
        on La Rue de Charonne,
a moonless sky
the remnants of a meal.
A waiter writes the menu on a board.

Marionettes stare
from the shop across the road.
A man walks four dogs at a time.
        Even in the rain
no one hurries on the streets of Paris.

A woman with fingerless gloves
sells flowers by the Seine,
now gray and lifeless
        impatient for Spring,
where doves make love
on gilded panes
and chimes cut the mist
like a delicate sickle.

There is a table by the window
        on La Rue de Charonne.
A girl holds a cat
like a lamb in her arms.
The spiral staircase behind the bar
        leads nowhere.
A thin cigarette
hand rolled from a pouch,
a glass of Tavel Lafond.

Parchment paper
and indigo ink.
        A letter
that will join the others
in the drawer of the bedside table
        at the Hotel Jules Caesar
where the pipes creak and rattle at night
like an ocean liner at sea.

R.G. Cantalupo
Almost Flying

(after Amichai)

If, just once, we could've made
a flying machine, or at least
a winged creature of some kind,
glided light as a kite over
that dark spine of mountains
beyond our bedroom window
or even floated like shadowy
zeppelins along our candlelit walls.
But whenever we tried we fell deeper
into the black hole of our bodies,
became spiders, beetles, worms,
rootbound things burrowing
inside the belly of earth, hungry.

No, even our best design—the one
we kept coming back to—looked
more like a grasshopper than
a bird. Still, for almost an hour,
we could be happy like that, bounc-
ing from shoot to shoot, my thigh
rubbing madly against yours, now
and then a sound rising, a high note
made of friction, a cricketlike song.

John Casey
Barbie and Ken in the Garden of Eden

Imagine how stiffly she must have reached for that apple,
how difficult it must have been to grasp.
We can almost see her head twisting in weak denial of temptation.
Of one thing we are certain:
that her freshly-minted flesh was beautiful;
the paradigm of curves, the genesis of symmetry.
We can imagine her frustration in that first moment of enlightenment
to not find a mirror hanging amidst the trees.

Imagine also his first taste of that new world,
fruit falling from his grasp with those first swellings of desire.
He wants to frame her nakedness in clothes, luxury cars, houses;
yet his empty hands are full of *not enough*.
Being unfamiliar with want, she is concerned by the look in his eyes,
the one that seems to stare past her sometimes,
but she moves closer anyway:

Design is irresistible.
Her skin is teleology. His shoulders are buildings.
Their hands reach towards infinite hungers.
Together, they watch the sun set on their last sleek and unblemished day,
smiles frozen against the slow revelation now snaking into their thoughts:
Forever hollow in jigsaw places.
Forever paired in assembly line existence.
Forever waiting for a world to outgrow.

Carlota Caulfield
Tres cuentos chinos

I. Espejo de metal

Un antiguo cuento chino
habla de un tal emperador Ts'in Shi (259-210 a.C.)
que poseía "el precioso espejo que iluminaría los huesos del cuerpo",
también conocido como "el espejo que ilumina la bilis".
El espejo aparece descrito como sigue:
rectangular de cuatro pies de ancho, cinco pies
            /y nueve pulgadas de alto,
brillante tanto en su interior como en su exterior.
Cuando alguien ponía las manos sobre su corazón,
observaba en el espejo sus vísceras.
Cuando un hombre se paraba ante él para ver su reflejo,
su imagen aparecía fragmentada en diminutos círculos.
De acuerdo con otra leyenda, era un pedazo de madera
sacada de un árbol llamado "el rey de los químicos".

II. Papalotes como pájaros

En un comentario de los *Anales de los libros de Bambú*
el emperador chino Shu es descrito como "ser volador",
"primer hombre que descendió sano y salvo en un paracaídas"
y "el que volaba como un pájaro".
Asciendo a la torre y no puedo descender,
mi padre le ha pegado fuego y todo se desploma. Era el siglo XII.
Gracias a mi buena cabeza y a mis dos sombreros de paja,
sombrillas útiles en cualquier circunstancia,
me tiro y aterrizo en tierra, con mi vestido de hilo en plena forma.
En definitiva, a pesar de las conspiraciones de mis hermanos,
siglos después Leonardo da Vinci me ha dejado trazado
en una de sus muchas libretas de aviación.
Después el veneciano Fausto Veranzio, ¿era acaso el siglo XVI?,
hizo varios trazos arrebatados y modificó el diseño.
Debo aclarar que el verdadero descenso de alguien en un paracaídas
no sucedió hasta 1783 en Montpellier.
Mis conocimientos de geografía son escasos,
y los nombres extranjeros me marean, pero aún así,
debo reconocer que los libros de historia
a veces dicen algunas verdades,
y además, yo estaba allí. En plena forma.

III. Yü min o aquellos que vuelan

Algunos escritores chinos cuentan sobre un país de seres voladores,
una isla cerca de un océano desconocido,

donde los veranos son muy calurosos,
y los habitantes viven en altas montañas
al lado del mar.
Algunos escritores chinos describen a los habitantes
de esta isla como seres con mandíbulas largas,
narices como picos de pájaro, ojos rojos, cabezas blancas
cubiertas con pelo y plumas, capaces de volar
pero no a largas distancias.
Muchos se arriesgan a lanzarse a lo desconocido,
pero la isla siempre se burla de ellos,
y a los que tratan de volar muy alto
los transforma en basura podrida.
Pocos son los que por puro milagro
cuando tratan de ascender al cielo
son transformados en inmortales,
llamados los "huéspedes de plumas"
expresión china que significa
monje taoista.

No puedo seguir con los cuentos chinos,
porque el emperador me podría mandar a matar.

Three Chinese Stories

I. Metal mirror

An ancient Chinese story
tells of a certain emperor, Ts'in Shi (259-219 B.C.)
who possessed "the precious mirror that will illuminate
        /the bones of the body."
Also known as "the mirror that illuminates the bile."
The mirror appears described as follows:
a rectangle four feet wide by five feet nine inches high,
both its interior and its exterior gleaming.
By putting their hands over their hearts, anyone
could see his viscera in the mirror.
When a man stood in front of it to see his reflection,
his image would appear fragmented into tiny circles.
According to another legend, it was a wooden board
from a tree called "the king of chemists."

II. Kites like birds.

In a commentary in the *Anals of the Bamboo Books*
the Chinese emperor Shu is described as a "flying being,"
"the first man to descend safe and sound in a parachute,"

and "the one who flew like a bird."
I climb the tower and cannot descend;
my father has set it on fire and everything is collapsing. It was
            /the 12th century.
Thanks to my good head and my two strew hats,
that provide useful shade in any situation,
I leap off and land on the earth, with my linen tunic spotless.
Definitively, despite my brothers' conspiracies,
centuries later Leonardo da Vinci left me sketched
in one of his many aviation notebooks.
Later the Venetian Fausto Veranzio, perhaps in the 16th century?,
made a number of impulsive brush strokes and modified the design.
I should state that no true descent by parachute
occurred until 1783 in Montpellier.
My knowledge of geography is slight,
and foreign names make my head swim, but even so,
I should acknowledge that history books
sometimes contain some truths,
and besides, I was there. Spotless.

III. Yü min or those who fly

Some Chinese writers tell of a country of flying beings,
an island near an unknown ocean,
where summers are very hot,
and the inhabitants live in high mountains
beside the sea.
Some Chinese writers describe the inhabitants
of this island as beings with large jaws,
noses like bird beaks, red eyes, white heads
covered with hair and feathers, capable of flying
but not for long distances.
Many dare to hurl themselves into the unknown,
but the island always mocks them,
and those who try to fly high up
are transformed into rotten garbage.
Few are those who by pure miracle,
upon attempting to ascend into the sky
are transfored into immortals
called the "feathered guests,"
a Chinese expression that means
Taoist monk.

I cannot continue with the Chinese stories
Because the Emperor might order me killed.

Translated by Mary G. Berg in collaboration with the author.

Jeanette Clough
The Day's Space

Between us is the day's space that our words, a glance, or picture
must pass through. And so we are displaced

the way the Amazon reaches for the Congo, or Italy's vineyard thigh
remembers watering the Sahara's flank.

My descant tongue prized the sand,
scrolling the dunes same as breakers. Weather took that balance away,
some tilt of axis turning wet to dry.

I'll take you where I am now, into the shift.
Nothing is where it appears to be: those stars,

far from their first light. It takes so long
to see. Or rather, the farther apart, the longer
your desired image travels to me in waves.

Viewed another way, the *nothing*

is exactly where it appears to be: in the blind spot
given for reference, a place of non-vision against which
the rest is seen. Better to scan than stare
in case I barnacle myself to a clumsy galleon
that sank ages ago with no chance of surfacing.

Or maybe you were never near, and I imagined the place completely.

Was it the soluble crystal of my salty desire, or hard mineral fact?

I'll never know without a deep dive
to prove whether the nothing is truly there,
or if under all that heavy water is a lost city
whose paving stones set end to end point to Bermuda,
Crete, or the liquid road to Skye.

Marcia Cohee
April Quartet

i   So it's Thursday already. Thursday,
with its dim light and cigarette smoke
and nail parlors where people like us
have forgotten Van Gogh's mad French
of wheatfields and crows
and heavy midnight skies,
though the picture is right there,
on the wall, above us.
And we tap dance through war
the same way
because people like us
have forgotten war too, this
shadow calling upon birds
we do not name, upon dinosaurs
unfeathered in the heat of space.

ii   Even the sand, forgetful sand, blows
as we crawl the night home.
I can hear tap shoes
and see the ballet underneath
it all, soundless
as a knife through water.

iii   Lozenge on the mind.
Trains, bridges
where we used to wait,
drowned for love, or not.
The coming apart of things:
faith, a stone, simmering.
Raise it to a boil, this soup
of numb belief.
And starve.

iv   Our daughters
practice their hearts' ballet.
Chairs on the balcony
are a little Paris, a little Saigon.
A fan cuts
through the light
which shimmers
on its shiny blades,
and we chat next door
in the nail salon,
generations away
from desperate boats and bicycles.
Generations with no memory
ahead of the moon.

Wanda Coleman
Daddyboy

1

with papa walking toward sunset
along the old railroad tracks in watts off 103rd
i am five in braids and bangs
and the blue cornflower print jumper mama made
the sun, a big copper smile
peeks over thunderheads
papa holds my tiny brown hand in his huge
boxer's fist. we wave at the switchman as we
walk past. i skip to keep in his giant's step
kicking granite pebbles as i go
watching them skitter in our path
home to mama

2

me & brother George have been up to mischief
we think we can outrun Daddyboy
and break for the front door. he runs us round
the house twice then passes us, laughing
we uh-oh surprise, stop in our tracks
and run back the other way
he spins round, catches us, holds me
in the vise of his calves as he
plucks George high into the air
and takes the tar out of us

3

Daddyboy surprises Mommygirl
with fats domino's latest hit, Honey Chile
they go into a clinch/kiss and we start to sniggle
they put it on the Victrola and
show us how to boogie woogie and Lindy Hop

we ooh ahh as he flips her over his back
and swings her between his legs
then they put on something slow
and send us off to bed

4

"Daddyboy Daddyboy Daddyboy's home!"
we run to greet him

"don't call me that no more!" his bass
is sharp and harsh. we run crying to Mommygirl
"your father's black. white people
disrespect black men by calling them boy
call him anything but"

5

we've been fighting. mom's gonna tell pop
our rear ends ache in anticipation
another whipping. mom uses a peach tree limb
all pop needs is those big powerful black hands
home, he lectures us. brother and sister
should love and respect. at 10 & 12
we're too big for such nonsense

George gets his first.
i figure a way to save my butt. i stuff my britches
with a book wrapped in a towel like i saw
on TV. George is hot tears and snot. it's my turn
WHOP WHOP WHOP. i fake a boo hoo
"what's this?" surprised he reaches in, pulls out
the towel. the book thuds to the floor.
he laughs and laughs so hard
he's almost crying and spanks me at the same time
and i'm laughing and crying and we're
laughing together
and shit does it hurt

6

one terrible morning pop came home in a sweat
he'd gone to the shop as usual
everything was gone. the printing presses
the desks. the files. the ledges. every damn thing
his partner had ripped him off

"what we gonna do? mom wailed
"i don't know" he said real quiet
i went hot and cold
he paced the room, slammed open the door
and went back to the streets

it is the only time i've ever seen him cry
and they was killin' tears

7

the phone screams. i jump up from my sleep
it's mama. can i come? papa's fallen
against the bathroom door. she can't get it open
she doesn't know if he's hurt
it's the seizures again brought on by scar tissue
from where they removed the tumor. yes
i'm on my way. and as i'm about to leave
the phone rings again. no
i don't have to come. the boys are coming
she says

but i go anyway

8

i take my father to the hills of Zion
for Wednesday night prayer meet
i'm long since a woman

he's long since grayed and grandfather
he goes into his wallet for the card and gives
it to me, his hands swollen/cushionoid
with illness. perhaps i'd like to come some time?
when i'm not too busy? they have a good choir.
i take the card, say okay say maybe
and wait patiently as he struggles
to get out of the car with the aid of his cane
and makes his way toward the light
of the open door

Classified Ads, May 1, 1608

2410 COUPLES THERAPY
Let me not to the marriage of true minds admit impediments. Love is not love.
2570 TAILOR / DRY CLEANER
Which alters when it alteration finds, or bends with the remover to remove; o, no! it is an ever-fixed mark.
2600 MARINE WEATHER
That looks on tempests and is never shaken; It is the star to every wandering bark.
2780 APPRAISALS
Whose worth's unknown, although his height be taken.
2810 COSMETICS
Love's not Time's fool, though rosy lips and cheeks.
2920 FARM IMPLEMENTS
Within his bending sickle's compass come.
3130 ESCHATOLOGY
Love alters not with his brief hours and weeks, but bears it out even to the edge of doom.
3355 EDITORIAL SERVICES
If this be error and upon me proved, I never writ.
4080 WOMEN SEEKING MEN
Nor no man ever loved.

Brendan Constantine
Last Night I Went to the Map of the World and I Have Messages for You

America says it has misplaced your number.
I wasn't comfortable giving it out. I said
I'd let you know.

Africa's Birthday is this weekend.
There's a party. No gifts.
                    Just come.

If you're planning to go, Greece wants
to know if it can get a lift. Awkwardly
                              so does Turkey.

Russia wanted me to say *The worm knows
the cabbage but the worm dies first.*
I have no idea what that means. Do you?

Japan looked really uncomfortable all night
but never spoke. Is something going on?

Ireland asked to be remembered.
I sang to it for you.

I didn't get to connect with Europe
but, as the French say, *Isn't that just*
                              too bad.

Is that everyone? Oh yes, the oceans.
They asked what they always ask
and I promised I'd repeat it,
                    Why do you never call?
                    When are you coming home?

Rachel Dacus
Disease Becomes the Last Panda

I wanted to hear that he was improving:
slowly becoming apt at puzzles,
less inclined to grab or say aloud, *waitress ass.*
I wanted to see his wrinkles stretch back
into the green New Jersey suburbs of 1948,
smooth as the gessoed canvas he stood before
under a single lightbulb, house still smelling
of paint and gypsum. I wanted my father to call
me when he said he would, just once
but the phone was heavy with his wife's
evasions and complaints of his inability to screw
on a jar lid. Is it that her English is slightly imperfect
or that I wanted him to be perfect again.
It was a disease to let myself think
of what comes next: the police
calling to ask if he resides there, or
worse, not calling.

His disease becomes increasingly the last
impression of him when I hang up.
It becomes the last panda
in a dilapidated tropical zoo
under new mismanagement, underfunded.
I want to save a whole species but cannot
even keep a clear picture of my father, pipe
lolling from his red-lipped grin
as he scatted to Satchmo
and *ba-da-ba-da-be-de-bahed*
across the empty studio.

Now I'm dating my memories, noting
them on bamboo leaves whose veiny scrawl,
impossible to read, is slowly munched
by the starving beast.

Ruth Daigon
Lost Landscapes

And the blind
whisper to each other
in thin voices.

They walk the borders of day
every street a new language
in a landscape already lost.

Hours slide by
smooth as polished chrome
and old habits are lovely

with memory coating fingertips
feet tracing the pavement's
rough language, and gravity

always underfoot. Faces turned toward
sun, they drink the rich, sweet
light and dream raw dreams

inside their world of black dazzle.
In survivors sad reckonings
they conjure names with one hand

and release them with the other
balancing on tightropes of sound.
And always a honed silence

as they carry solitude up the stairs
where time is a slow thought
and forever just another possibility.

They ask her to describe darkness.
she begins with the charred edge
of the sea, winds trapped in caves, a wheel

turning away from itself. She has
gone into the hollow place
behind her eyes, to the outer edge

of sight moving on white lizard feet.
No longer blinded by the visible,
the world is nearer in the dark.

J. P. Dancing Bear
Fog Through a Bridge

for Ralph Angel

Because your body has become fog
rearranging the constellations,
coating the leaves with your breath—
say it's not hard to remember
the incantations that made you this, now.
How many times was smoke written about?—
coursing, billowing up the mirror
toward a reflection you'd never intended.
An isolated girl has written a love sonnet
to your ocean. She's corked the bottle
and thrown it off the bridge.
She counts the seconds
it takes to splash the water,
as if she were mouthing the words
he loves me, he loves me not.

Tonight the skyline is stained
by fire and sirens,
but you focus on the gulls' cries
and the fog horn tearing through you—
a warning, a wicked something
comes this way.
No one sleeps within your arms.
A man sings a drunken love song
which you've heard before,
only backwards or jumbled.
A woman looks at you
like an old friend and you roil.
The immigrants have closed
their shops for the night. Traffic horns
call out like carnival barkers.
You cradle the city like a child
found abandoned on the back step.
No one hears the lullaby you offer
except the alley cats
and one girl counting on a bridge.

Lori Davis
On A Scale Between 1 and 10 (10 Being Best)

I dug into the wind and didn't stop until I found
my breath, a changing length of bluish mist.
On a scale between 1 and death (death being best),
tell me, why should we calm this rush?

I was led around by lust and didn't stop
until I'd been rounded smooth, a noseless stone.
On a scale between 1 and teeth (teeth being worst),
tell me, how should we mesh this thirst?

I littered inside a dream and didn't stop until I filled
your cellophane heart. A dream, invisible farce.
On a scale between 1 and nowhere (nowhere being here),
tell me, how far should we escort this fear?

I talked to myself inside the earth and didn't stop
until I reached your stony eyes and liquid ears.
On a scale between 1 and truth (truth being next),
tell me, how can we deepen this depth?

Tomás Esteban de San Andreas
We

We northward slink at night,
a swarm of shadows.
Bronze bodies spill
over the border,
slide and freeze
on sand dunes,
then spurt and scatter
like cockroaches
between the lights
of lurking patrol.

We bend to plant and pick
lettuce and artichokes and grapes.
We clean up yards,
haul trash in beat-up trucks.
We dust pianos
and mind other people's
wealthy children.
We disappear
when someone looking official
is spotted nearby.

Burden-bellied women,
with broods of bright-eyed urchins
clinging to their skirts,
carry bags of food
from San Antonio de Padua.
In crowded quarters
with cardboard in the window,
we cook our meals
of beans and maize,
hot chili and chorizo,
as it has been our custom.

We speak with hands
and helpless grins
in shy, insistent phrases.
We learn and toil,
we drink and fight
and fill the jails,
where burdened-bellied women
with broods of bright-eyed niños
come to visit.

We see what others have,
and somewhere
between hope and resignation
we spend our nights
in study or in stupor,
between the twilight of today
and troubles of tomorrow . . .

Nita Donovan
Is That All There Is

Is that all there is
this parking lot
of loneliness?

You think I can make you feel
young again, hide determined death,
love you?

Who said, after the kiss
comes the impulse to throttle?

Is that romantic enough for you?
I don't say any of this.

He wants to walk the beach
but not alone.
He wants to meet me anywhere,
maybe at Starbucks.

I want to ask, aren't you strong
enough to live alone?
But I don't.

I tell him, I never go out,
don't want to hurt his feelings.

He says, well if you're not interested
what about your friend,
what about Roberta?

Diane Dorman
My Heroes

In high school it was the slim-hipped,
broad-shouldered quarterback,
that fluttered my pom poms
or the leather-jacket, bad boy
hair slicked back in a D.A.,
that made my poodle skirt pant.

But after 35 years of marriage
in an old house
with leaky pipes, rusty hinges
and a cracked façade,
it's the man with the tool belt
slung low on his hips
strutting like Gary Cooper in High Noon
that makes me sigh.
Step aside Robert Redford
make way for the Maytag Repairman
he's not lonely anymore.
Superman and Spiderman dis the tights.
My super hero's in paint-splattered denim
and a sweaty, cotton tee
sawdust on his eyebrows
and axle grease under his nails,
saw buzzing in the garage
work boots pounding on the roof.
A little bit of butt-crack's a bonus
as he hunkers in the cavern under the sink
making all my household dreams come true.

ellen
Your Back Grew Large

for Herb

your back so large
it holds
back mud

holds back hunks
of wall
and sliding roof

mud slides
over us
all the houses gone

all the houses
leveled
bits of stick and grass

we pick each other
clean
like arboreal gibbons

we pick each
dried mud piece
a last prison meal

uncover our nakedness
your front
your tender front

Carrie Etter
The Bonds

for Matt

What wharf has neither metal anchor nor heavy coils of rope?
Farther down the Thames is a bridge once favoured
by prostitutes for its low guardrail, the ease of descent,
though other, unmentioned girls came to prop a heel
on its cold steel and so divulge a shapely calf.

Which is to say that a search of the dock would find the usual
instruments of restraint, but of such strange material
that though their forms would foster recognition, you'd yearn
to touch them, to weigh in a palm the anchor that could not
pin a bird, the rope as light as a mouthful of fruit.

Hard science might explain the boat's fidelity by reckoning the waves'
relative stillness, the craft's weight, the distance of the moon.
And as for "soft" science, the –ologies of more elusive chemistries,
leave them to speak amongst themselves with a shrug
of your pale shoulders, with the memory of one deepening kiss.

Marcia Falk
Counting Birds

Nine birds on nine twigs
at the top of the orange-leafed maple
fifty yards from my window.
Now ten. Now seven. Now nine again.

The rain cleaned the leaves from the tips of the branches,
leaving a spot for a bird on each one.

Eight. Five. Now only four—
perched in twos, sitting still,
balanced,
a pair on each side of the tree,
their twin silhouettes etched crisply in the pearl-gray sky.

But here comes one more, tilting the picture to the right,
and now the one in the middle flaps her wings
and off she goes—
off—

From the windowed distance, the shifting calligraphy of birds
is indecipherable,
meaningless.
Still, because I am human, I imbue it with signs:
Five make a dark abstraction—
mystery on mystery.
Three—
Ah, the poetic starkness of three.
Two and two—
another story altogether.

Sister Linda says birds are angels.
She is not being metaphorical.
She says a bird will come to her
in times of distress or indecision
and tell her what to do.
If one comes, she knows to choose yes.
And if one doesn't come, I ask,
do you choose no?
I might still choose yes, she answers.

Oh, there are so many languages
I cannot read,
each an unashamed, beautiful darkness
even in its radiance.

Jay Farbstein
Behind the Nostril

Given a certain alignment of nostril, mirror and sun
reflected from behind the viewer, it is sometimes possible
to see the entire universe revolving inside the skull.

He, for example, once spotted his father, miraculously without
a cane, pitching a softball game. And on another occasion
saw the entire 7th Fleet mothballed in Suisun Bay

with the Golden Gate Bridge and Angel Island in the background,
luminous in the afternoon light. At other times all he could see
was a child lying on its back in a crib, absent-mindedly

toying with a live cat suspended on a string. But at times it is
impossible to see past the bristling hairs—and they appear
to be the remnants of a wooden door blasted off its hinges

by the force of a life reinventing itself. And the splinters,
stuck deep into the flesh on passing through the door,
feel excruciatingly painless and entirely deserved.

Ann Fisher-Wirth
Blue Window

In that shadowy time before sorrow—
that twilight, October in Berkeley, the early 60's,

when I walked home along Euclid from Mrs. Runkle's
where I'd played Schumann's *Traumerei*

so beautifully, for once, I'd made her cry—
Before the missile crisis, when I sat on the bed in fear and exaltation

and thought of Anne Frank—while on the TV downstairs,
Soviet ships inched closer to Cuba—and wondered,

when they come to get me, when I hide beneath my desk,
my head in my hands, and the walls shake,

will I have told the world
how I love this life I am forced to lose?

Before Christian, my neighbor, drank developing fluid
and his death at Alba Bates took 48 hours, the poison dissolving his stomach,

and his father the beautiful philanderer told my mother,
"The divorce caused it," just failing to add, wringing

his elegant crooked fingers, "He did it for grief of me"—
before Ronnie, my neighbor, took acid and flew out a window,

and Jackie, my neighbor, drove 90 miles an hour into a stone wall
at prep school in Massachusetts, and Kwaasi, my neighbor,

talked to God and carved his arms and died at Napa,
the boys who lived around me lost, all dead by nineteen—

and before I had ever bled yet, ever got high, or
loved a boy, or played at kisses through Kleenex with Mary Lou—

In that time before my father lay in bed
all one year's end, the vast flower of his death blossoming,

and wrote, in a tiny crabbed hand, in the datebook I found years later,
"Had to increase the dosage today. Ann and Jink allowance"—

in that Christian Science household no one spoke,
to this day no one has ever said to me, "It was brain cancer,"

but last winter my husband got drunk in his rare blind fury,
ran weeping into the room and pounded the bed over and over,

shouting, "Don't you understand yet?
In the war they treated men for lice with Lindane,

poured it over their heads,
they did it to your father, and now the fuckers tell us

Lindane eats your brain."—In that time, that twilight,
when I walked slowly home along Euclid,

how I wanted to belong to the family I saw
through the blue, wisteria-covered window, to be their girl,

enter their garlicky dinnertime kitchen,
later, to sit on a high attic bed, legs crossed tailor-fashion,

and pick dreamily at white chenille—
I wondered, why not be anyone, go anywhere?

When light dies around the oak leaves
and white, ragged moths come out to beat against the streetlight,

why not knock at the door and say, "I am yours. I am here"?

Michael C. Ford
On My Way to See You

But they don't cancel the tickets
anymore: they cancel the whole goddam

train. Whether far in a Coyote Point or
just a bit North of Coronado Isle, we are

disguised by torrey pines: their mischievous
dust makes miniature sandcastles in our

noses. Now we're looking into the drone
of a navy plane: its jets devour the sky. Oh

go away: no it has to be a transport: one of
those RKO process shots: a 1940's replica

could get us registered in this haunted hotel
at sea edge. Every man in the lobby looks

at you not unlike the Bowery Boys all in love
with Dona Drake: or maybe the prodigality

of Kirk Douglas giving it up for his "dear
secretary" Laraine Day who will not be

dictated to by anybody. However, here's my
trip: simply being on my way to see you:

except for the fact that you happen to be
remarkably already here.

Amélie Frank
Pumpkin Confidential

For Laurel Ann Bogen and Erica Erdman

Harrumph! This is no smile.
This is a rictus of negative space,
and I am growing surly in my old age
What is retirement? Sulking for days
on a west-facing slope above Half Moon Bay
among the rest of the failed carriages?

I should have been more than the scullery gal's ride home.
I should have been the centerpiece of the ball,
not the rolling, rolling, rolling means to the anteroom.
I don't care that the punch
would have poured out my eyes.
So what? Pedigree?
My children are these flat teardrops,
dried out, salted, sold at
the counter with ginseng packs and quick picks.

Advice: never work with other harbingers of the season.
Cats especially, and most especially if they are
a spinster's familiar. The little bastards are
prone to devour the landscape,
amplifying desire,
snatching the very breath from the sky.

Skeletons, on the other hand, have it easy
this time of year. October sees them heading south
on noisy party busses for the festivities in San Antonio,
Cabo, and Miami. Call them the xylophone people.
When they dance, every step is a windchime's report.

October finds me finishing out my days
as a smudge pot. Near the witching hour,
the pubescent runts, lacking soap, will make merry
by hurling me at the grumpy farmer's front porch.
Put it to together and what have you got?
A boneyard of pulp and only 55 shopping days left
until you-know-what—*that's what!*

Albert Garcia
Frog Eggs

They started as a small slime
of black dots. After
wading through the pond,
you and the boys
carried in a plastic bucket,
poured brackish water
into a clear bowl, and there
they were, a little jelly packet
of lives that grew daily
under our magnifying glass.
They're turning flat,
you tell me as you peer in
this afternoon, and I admit
I'm as caught up in this
as the boys who announce
any wiggle, any sign
that the tail, legs, gills
will come. But I'm content
to watch you watch the eggs, you
hovering over the bowl,
hair encircling your face
like dark ferns surrounding a pool
below a waterfall,
holding, accentuating the
light.

Richard Garcia
Dreaming of Sheena

The sun wiped out the night like an eraser.
It was a morning fit for pancakes
but my lucidity found no outlet.
So I went back to my dream, a groovy
dream of love, adventure and terrorism
and Sheena of the Jungle in her underwear.

Sheena had skimpy, leopard-skin underwear.
Her thonged behind emptied my mind like an eraser.
Then, out of frustration, I became a terrorist
with explosives disguised as pancakes
and plastiques in my shoes that were groovy.
My mission: blow up the Eddie Bauer Outlet.

Or was it the Citadel or the Desert Hills Outlet?
I had ammunition stashed in my underwear.
It made me walk bow-legged but I felt groovy.
After a series of explosions I craved pancakes.
But they tasted like warmed-over pencil erasers.
I wanted to dream of love not terrorism.

Or was dreaming of love a kind of terrorism?
But dreams of love were not the way out.
Let me find a woman with the scent of pancakes.
I searched for a phone number over and under.
Where could it be, I hope I didn't erase
her number from existence. Then—groovy

and cool, I found it and let me repeat, groovy!
I tried to focus and dial but I was in terror.
Isms of doubt crossed my heart like erasers
on a blackboard. Would I find an outlet
for my jungle passion sniffing her underwear?
Or was she really just ugly under her pancake

makeup? Could I be the one to butter her pancakes?
May her thighs snap shut on me! Here follows groovy
fantasies of Sheena underwater in her underwear,
Sheena with knife between teeth, Sheena fights terrorism,
while I toss and turn, wishing for an outlet—
here follow galloping zebras striped black and white like erasers.

Would I wake to pancakes or love like terrorism?
Would I wake yelling groovy or take me to the outlet!
May our underwear spin together or from my dreams erase her.

John Gardiner
No Ships Left to Steer

When darkness locks like a holding cell and jail bars writhe like
snakes, when breath is short and humans don't understand—seek out
those who simply feel, avoid all others; visit backyard jungles
in the mind, lie down with dogs and dig for seeds of memory,
dream of elephants who pass the bones of elders from trunk to trunk
and sadly, fondly reminisce…study love with canines—
when lonely as a mourning dove that's lost its mate, never to mate again,
gone to a grave of enduring drought, turn again to dogs…umbilical links to
instinct, scruff-haired angels at your feet…always turn to dogs because
wolf and coyote won't come near, and the moon's a lonely beacon
with no ships left to steer.

Katya Giritsky
Planting Grandma

like Neanderthals
we put violets in your hands

and when it was all over
we couldn't just leave you
suspended over astroturf

but they hadn't expected
for us to say yes
we want to see her lowered
and they had to scurry about
until they found two gardeners
who knew how to work the lift

so we stood around
watching Paco and Rames
lower you into the ground
and I kept thinking

you always loved gardens
you would have wanted
to have gardeners plant you

Terry Godbey
Fourteen

We were most smitten
the first days of summer,
stretched out on our blankets
like the three months before us,
skin shimmering with coconut concoctions,
leaving greasy prints on *Seventeen* models.
Boys patrolled nearby, hoping to glimpse
the cocktail waitress
who answered the door in her bra
or waiting for long games of Twister,
faces so close, our bodies striking like matches.

Sticky and throbbing, we paraded to the pool
for its slap of icy water, me in my first bikini,
hot pink, with its hedge of chaste lace
my mother sewed on.
Only my breasts swam, the wet trim fallen,
boys holding their breath
and parting the water for close-ups,
their fish eyes red.

The sun slid down the sky's throat
like butterscotch, summoning us
to the street light for hide-and-seek.
Sam Hanson, star of my diary, shouted
I'm gonna kiss the last girl I find
and I ran, forgot about snakes and crouched,
pebbles tattooing my palms,
my breathing so loud
I feared it might give me away
too soon.

Gotcha.
The hairs on my arms stood up and cheered
and even with eyes closed I saw
what lay ahead, a tilting fun house
and no place to hide,
ready or not.

Jessica Goodheart
Instructions for the House Sitter

I.

To be thrown in the black container by the curb:
carcasses picked clean, torn blouses,
knives bent beyond repair.
Always the trash collectors come
with their early Tuesday morning
reproaches. Pay them no mind.

II.

Best not interfere with the plants.
They are engaged in a civil war,
root against root. Daily, vegetation
comes into this world unnamed.

III.

Ignore the alarm that sounds nightly,
the Doppler effect from sirens approaching,
the police officers with their
nightsticks and clean shaves.
They will ask for the code.
It is *Judas*. Do not tell them.

IV.

Refill the dog's dish in the evening.
But do not walk him unless
you are prepared to go as he does,
on all fours, weathering bloody knees,
hours of solitude.

V.

The cat, once out of the house,
will climb to the neighbor's roof.
You will hear him cry.
He cannot get down.
The rain will start,
winds will tear down the power lines,
the whole hillside will go dark.

Jessica Goodheart
Vanishing

Did I tell you about our room, how it's growing smaller? Each day, we lose an inch, I figure.
It creeps up on you the way a perfectly lovely evening fades to night. At first, we thought
clutter made the room cramped. I put magazines at right angles, lined up lotions and
mascara like little soldiers. Life returned to almost normal. We even made love
once, bumping together in the hot, small room. The next time: too hot, too
small. Soon we were pushing the dresser into the hall, discarding plants
we'd nurtured from seed. People have made do with less: Dad, as
a kid, slept in the living room, Grandma always barging in on
him in the bathroom with fresh towels. Tried remodeling,
hired a company that organizes closets. But by the time
they arrived: walls only 3 ft apart husband after
me to lose weight no room for us both.
Since he left I feel better. Remarkable
how much room another person
can take. No furniture now but
when I sit with my back
against one wall feet
against the other I
form a per-
fect
V

S.A. Griffin
Genius

a dangerous word
full of guilt and promise
often misunderstood
much less if ever
defined or fulfilled

there is genius in ignorance
more than one could ever design
into the hysterical awe and wonder of the greatest bomb yet to be
or the mayhem of microscopic conclusion
franchised by the architects of fear

genius wears black
believes in the rubric crucible of death after death
rides the feral roller coaster of depression
arms raised high
and negotiates the aether of
falling dreams one foot in front of the other
with verse

calls history liar
and weeps openly over the most casual cliché
breathes art
bleeds light
befriends trees
and everything yet to know

wears the untrained hair of a nervous garden
and is learning to play Gershwin's Rhapsody
on Picasso's blue guitar

    when walking into a room
    most experience eggs, water, salt, sugar & flour

    others taste cake

Dina Hardy
Bacchus

You think life is all jazz and easy conversation
breathing through an open window as you pluck
another grape from the bunch in your fat fingers.
Flesh upon lip and roll the orb across your tongue
as if eating the Earth. Even as a child you smiled,
said, *more* and *again*.

I Get Along Without You Very Well, croons Billie Holiday.
I know she's lying.

A bottle tipped empty, another uncorked, glasses raised
to friends' first house, news of first child, promotion.
I want to forget that I'm renting, single,
unemployed. We're listening to *Lady in Satin*,
she's intoxicating and I'm beginning to feel the booze
mixing with blood, numbing thoughts
that I'm not immortal like you.

But *I'm glad to be unhappy* as the room slips
like fingers playing jazz piano. It's midnight...
four in the morning and oh my god,
Bacchus, I cannot feel my teeth, cannot say your name.
What have you done to my tongue? Slurring,
back sliding down the wall to the floor
to the cool linoleum against my face.

Bacchus—your name means twice born.
Within you lie the bestial and the sublime. The music
ended a long time ago but I can't hear the silence
over the blood pounding in my ears.
Curled by this dishwasher I sleep
and wait to be born again.

John C. Harrell
Epiphany

There is no sound, except Chopin's notes,
with crickets as a chorus.
Darkness hides all life.
A single light burns,
illuminating nothing.
Mind fills the void.
Memory records the event.

John Harris
England Up Close

A woman, woozy, fluttering from one free
sip to the next, a child, older than his
years, standing on his seat, watching,
dining on Kendalmint and handouts. "It's
me bye-bee!" she gushes, weaving through
the coach with swarms of dragon-clad Scots
on track to a soccer riot in Barcelona.
You're streaking Newcastle to London on
the Highland Bullet, three hundred miles
in three hours, the Midlands a dirty blur.

Last week you did three days, pub to pub,
around Troutbeck, Grasmere, Ambleside,
then all night in a drizzle on an ancient
postal lorry across Yorkshire moors, over
Ribbleshead Viaduct, close to the ruins
of Roman forts. You paused at Haltwhistle
to sample the tea and the lager in the twin
villages of Once Brewed and Twice Brewed.

Now you're nearing London. Eyes closed,
fingers crossed, the boy is singing softly
to himself. Maybe he's unburdening, asking
whoever it might concern for forgiveness
and mercy. Leaving St. Pancras Station
you notice sunfire on St. Paul's limestone.
At the British Museum you happen upon
the Magna Carta, the original Magna Carta.
"John by the grace of God, King of England,
to all faithful subjects, know that we, for
the salvation of our soul, do promise…."
Stunned and out of words, you go into tears
in plain view of the guard and of everyone.

Barbara Hauk
The Amaryllis

A red so intense it interrupted
me blazed outside your window.
"What is it?"

"An Amaryllis." Two days later, there
you both were, a plant's long tropical
leaves hanging out of the pot.

You cleared root space, packed dirt in
beyond my picture window, saying
the sprawl of leaves along the ground

would die back and a fresh
stem and flower emerge, two seasons
from now. Half-aware, I mark

its place daily, impatient
to repeat the startling new red. I have
sought lipstick that pure.

There is no such paint, even blood thins
to orange or darkens to blue.
A poinsettia is a sunburnt amaryllis.

If it were real fire, it would hold and spread.
But it will be contained: stiff and upright, still,
on its pale green stem;
though wind flows across the back yard,
this is a miracle of heat at a distance.

Susan Hecht
Why I Said Yes

He'd driven all night
to hand me the box,
a tiny coffin
with rings in velvet.
We met by a stream
trickling in the sun
whose light played the diamond
like a strobe
fragmenting his face.
I tried to see him clearly—
Aryan profile, determined chin—
as the top of my head baked.
Squirrels ran and hid.
I knew life with him would be
hard and wrong,
and my parents disapproved
of the goy and his unfinished education.
I buckled under
the memory of my mother
clinging
to her war-time soldier husband.
Behind her stood a crowd
of aunts and grandmothers
who ruled their houses
despite the crowns
on their husband's tired brows.
They speared me
with prongs on their large rings,
shut my books in their cupboards and
pushed me outside.
Stop being alone, they hissed,
You must have a man
who loves you.

Joy Harold Helsing
Jill Testifies

Yes, your honor, I know
I have to tell the truth.

On the morning it happened,
Mother wanted to make soup
so Jack and I set out
to fetch a pail of water
from the spring on the hill.
We noticed new gravel on the path
but didn't think anything of it.

Coming back downhill
with both of us holding the handle
all of a sudden those little round pebbles
started rolling under our feet. Jack fell,
the pail went flying, and I tumbled after.
I landed on my butt, just got bruised,
but Jack hit his head hard on a rock.
When I picked myself up and went to help,
he was all bloody. I couldn't wake him.

He was unconscious for two whole days.
It was really scary. Then he couldn't
remember what happened. The doctor called it
"traumatic amnesia." As if that weren't enough,
now he's terrified of pails. If we bring one near
he gets short of breath, sweaty,
his heart pounds fast, he's panicky.
So I have to fetch the water alone,
make two trips instead of one.
We're afraid he's going to be like this
the rest of his life.

Our lawyers say the town should pay
for Jack's medical bills, pain and suffering,
the extra work I have to do, the loss
of his future earning power. I think
that's only fair. Before the town council
fixed that path, they should have done
a risk assessment, traffic analysis,
and environmental impact study.
We're holding the mayor
personally responsible.

Marvin R. Hiemstra
It's Only Cellular

All you need
is a throw away
pink
flamingo
phone
in the palm
of your
sweet hand.

Humans chat each other up all day long
on their double guarantee cling free flip-phones.

Men's eager to please *you know whats*
shoot for the Stars while their owners mutter

sweet nothings into devious little cellulars.
"I'm in line at the Post Office right now

so I can't.... Ohhhhh! Me, too! Ohhhhh,
Baby!" All day long those hard working

you know whats aim valiantly at the Ozone.
Trying to keep a straight face Mona Lisa Sun

carefully counts them, blows each
a hot kiss, and blushing dies: laughing.

Finally late at night—it has been the longest day—
those humans meet, face to face, and the lights

go low and those totally exhausted *you*
know whats can no longer point to the Stars

who shout down, high on Cosmic Glee,
"WHO'S SORRY NOW?"

Larkin Higgins
Casting Signs

The fishermen wait, then ignore the no overhead casting sign. *No Tire*
El Cordel Por Arriba. There has been such a urgency to trace the sun's

fall. Its edges bleed the sea. Fragments of fishing line curl like hair left
at the bottom of the tub you so neatly wiped after our afternoon bath.

Our time has been about water—crossing the ocean to meet and meet
again, washing our words, trying to merge two languages. The wetness

as our syllables slide, rearrange themselves, find their correct positions.
But on this pier, I wait for the sun to dunk itself once more, slip into

the current and turn the world hot orange again. I expect it. This
navy blue water trembles for the descent. I watch halfway out of my body

for fear that sun's insertion will be too much for this cold water.
The buoys tip from side to side. I watch them balance. And remember
your

last message—Let's not talk of desire. And I think there is nothing
without desire, the swollen sun's bulge, the hazy horizon, that sharp

glitter line the sun makes.

Christine Holland
What They Ate: Mission San Jose, 1800

After the *Padres* came and built their mud houses
where they said, *Dios vive*, the people ate
God's body, a flat white thing with no flavor,
and more: they learned to grow wheat for bread,

tend cattle and sheep, eat tame fruit picked
from trees that grew where oaks had given acorns.
Livestock foraged the hills and meadows,
elk and deer grew lean on small rations, or fled.

Rivers that had always gone their own way
were directed into ditches, ponds, sent
in channels to the fields where foreign grasses
claimed the ground. The people used to choose

their way like water; now they hauled boulders,
un trabajo pesado, and cleared canals of silt.
After such hard labor, the *Padres* promised,
they would rest in *El Cielo*, where no one

goes hungry, no one works, and *El Señor*
would give back all they had lost.
When they sickened and died in great numbers,
they were glad at least that once again

they would eat salmon and horn snails,
wild buckwheat and fennel, mussels
and blackberries, fiddleneck shoots,
the sweet oily acorn, baked on hot stones.

Nancy Hom
Breathing a Space for Memories

Memories are like pricks from corals
that leave bloody marks on our feet.
Time has not smoothed their sharp edges
but we have learned where to step
to avoid them.

Now our vast space of connection
has been reduced to a tunnel
from which sometimes crawls love, bewildered,
as if it does not know
it too belongs here.

Mother,
it is time to let the sting of memories
widen our narrowed space, so I may know
what depth of fire has forged my hand
into a steel fist, as I stand
before my cowering daughter.

I remember:
The whack of the chicken feather duster;
the pinches that left rainbow colors under my arms;
the darkness of the closet you locked me in;
the hisses of "ugly monkey" in my ear.

And this too:
Coming home from graduation,
my eyes wet-rimmed, eyebrows knitted in a V.
I curled into an angry knot and screamed,
"All the parents were there.
Except you."

It was I who did the yelling that time.
The English words you never mastered
created a wall between our worlds and left you
without a language
with which to pierce me.

There were spareribs smoking in the steamer;
plates of chicken and fish untouched.
I slammed the steel-plated door when I left,
the scent of roses from my corsage
still in the air.

Perhaps
your memories are not like mine.

You remember:
Years of sweat sewing in factories
blouse after blouse after blouse;
the thousands of beads patiently strung
into necklaces for white throats,
for your children's education.

You remember:
Snow peas drizzled in soy sauce and sesame;
beef sizzling in an old clay pot;
stuffed dumplings for the Sunday meal;
the choicest meats saved only for me.

Now you edge your way to the living room,
steadied by a thick wooden cane.
You brush aside yesterday's newspapers
from the faded rose-print couch.
The sofa still bears the imprint
of your body from the night before.
Slowly you try to fit into the exact same position
and wonder why
your children don't call you.

Three thousand miles away
I too sit, eyes half closed,
breathing a space that can include the memories.
The warmth of your back against my face;
the sorrow of the hand
that raged against the fate
that brought you here.

I breathe until there is breath for three.
With each inhalation we heave in unison.
A breath for my mother,
a breath for my daughter,
and a breath for me.

Angela Howe
Family Circle

At nine years old
I help my parents get stoned.
This is when they are still friends.
And dad has a coffee table
with a secret door
for his small stash of marijuana, matches,
and Zig-Zag papers.

While my mother lights candles and incense
like an abbess before evening mass,
he arranges his supplies with a precision
he lacks in ordinary life.

Like a surgeon or a master chef
he gently rolls a tight little cigarette.
Sometimes in silence.
Sometimes with a lesson:
The trick is to not overstuff the dooby.
I nod wisely, watch them
and plan a run to Taco Bell when they get hungry.

Soon, the house turns magical with lush, tangy smoke
whorls and whorls of it fanning from their mouths
spiraling from cones of incense
seeping from burning joints and orange candles.

I take my place by the record player,
wait for dad's signal.
First he hums, then:
Put on the Creedence, Boo

I play the album as he takes one more long hit
then sways into my mother's arms.
They rise like a marvelous dragon
exhaling in a kiss
while the band croons about hoodoo chasing
and Bayou queens.
They each take my hand and
we make a clumsy sort of circle
a silly sort of family
giggling and dancing like
the children we were meant to be.

Robin D. Hudechek
Ghost Walk

We used to overturn rocks on the shore
and expose them to the belly of the sun.
I knew that some rocks should not be moved
but you picked them up to skip pebbles
and slice fountains in the sea
where they were lost
and you were satisfied
because yours had skipped the farthest
and the deepest
while mine grew steam in my palm.

Your hand in mine was sandpaper,
When you closed your fingers I was a bottled neck
with no wings flapping but the heartbeat
of one chipped stone against another.

In the ocean your rosary curls the foam
and the stones fly all in pieces.
As the seaweed entwines your fingers, I wonder
if you walked alone as you promised
and if the water sipped your lips.

Under blankets, my feet are wet.
In the moonlight footprints pause on the shore
as if, in leaping, you turned. I imagine you found comfort
in the smaller hand that clung to yours,
in the transparent, almost unreal dress
that floated above her hair
then gave way, flattening against her legs
when you pushed her back.

Elizabeth Iannaci
Fountain and Vine

Even the janitor's gone home
leaving a chemical freshness
that invades like the cold.
This floor was Sinatra's refuge
in the Fifties, this frozen fireplace
witness to trysts with
those young ones—their tight
sweaters bursting with hope.
I imagine his lips smoothing
their pincurled hair, voice
soothing, soaking into their skin
like sunshine. The voice
that soundtracked a generation:
first-dated and goodbye-d
and *I'll be seeing you-ed*
soldiers and housewives
off to battle and the factory,
penny-loafered girls, hungry
for their boyfriends' furloughs,
and 4fer's, not too ashamed
to swing on a Friday night.
This was his sanctum sanctorum
atop the Studio. These French
windows grinned at a Hollywood
past its magic hour, a Hollywood
whose hookers hung blue
scarves over their red lights
to avoid the blacklist,
while film factory kitchens
baked smiles into apple pies.
He holed-up above it all and waited:
       for his horses to place
       for McCarthy to tarnish
       for the martinis to chill
until he became chairman of the bored
then packed his rats
for Palm Springs and clean air
leaving nothing but
his fingerprints,
the fireplace
and this empty lunchroom.

Thea Iberall
Abracadabra

Words.
Some words stay around forever. Others
barely an eyeblink.
Slang words like *daddio, groovy* or *rad*
get old-fashioned, come and go within
a generation. They're gone like your health
discarded as quickly as a friend who sleeps
with your lover when you go out of town.

Some words lose their reason for existence
bewray or *spinning jenny* or the name
I used to call you.
They get replaced, like friends are when we move
to a new town or the next passage in our evolution.
A *computer* used to be a job description.
Now it sits on your desk to document
the changes in your life.

Some words were there from the beginning.
I'm sure the first Englishmen
needed to speak of food and water and love
(before there was take out pizza and Perrier and betrayal).
These staple words are among the first we learn.
They stay around forever like college roommates
who won't disappear just because
you are getting a divorce
or going through chemo.

And then, there are the really old words
inherited from ancient times. Words like sorrow
which came from the Old German *sorega,* which grew
from *sraga,* an Old Slavic word meaning
sickness. They're so old you
don't know why they are there
like your friendship with your second grade
classmate who taught you to make
high pitched noises through your nose.
Words like *abracadabra*
which meant "perish like the word"
when it began its cabalistic journey nearly
3000 years ago on the banks of the Euphrates.
Perhaps it began one night as a Chaldean mother
tried to comfort her ailing daughter by a warm hearth.
As a game, perhaps, or a play on her name. She whispered

abbada ke dabra over and over, each time with
one less letter, telling her the pain would go
away with each discarded *a* and *r* until all
that was left were the low embers
and her child's sleeping form.

She smiled, just the way
you did, on the day you
said abracadabra and I
turned around and
you were
gone

Elijah Imlay
Ants

1

Because of a hoarse wind
I have a dry cough, and red ants
have withdrawn to their fortress
in a neglected cemetery.
I count chain links in the dark
as if I could see them, return
to the security fence as though
there were safety in a name,
and rub the facets of my
pendant because there are
no edges to this night.

The new moon gives no light,
so I'm safe from prying eyes.
Twice each hour War Dog and I
circle the ammo dump.
My pulse quickens as I flash
the dim filtered light, ghostly
red, checking for signs
of entry, barbed wire bent
or cut. We can be seen,
yet without this lamp I can't
see what am I stepping on.
Straggler ants?

2

The dog strays while he sniffs,
taking us through their foes,
large black ants that dwell
beyond a river of grass
in another citadel.

And my mind roams to a time
when I walked with my dad
into the dusk of scrub-covered hills
above John Day, Oregon,
where he flash-lit a space to pitch a tent.
At midnight, we woke to brush fires
spreading on our skin.
Mandibles dug trails.
Without larynx or tongue,
ants spoke through our cries.

Next day my brother, Marc,
kept a journal noting the colors
of head, thorax and abdomen
unique to each ant colony –
two red, one black – two black,
one red – all red, all black.
Then we saw an ant war:
red against black, eggs
being carried off, small ants
fastened to the legs
of larger ones, foot soldiers
cut up and hauled away.

3

War Dog rubs against me,
unfettered by collar or leash.
I straighten my dog tags
and pretend we're taking a stroll.
Checking a padlock, I know better,
but the dog is a comfort.
We're in the same pack.

What we guard – flares,
bullets, artillery rounds,
enough TNT to blast a crater
larger than the air field –
is not what scares me.

It's that new lieutenant
I saw pacing, his feet not yet
heavy from what he'll carry.
He wore a gold stripe, meaning
he's a West Point graduate
who would get men killed
for a rank reason. If we're lucky
he'll die doing a John Wayne.

It's the ear a soldier showed me
while in line for a flight.
One for each kill, like taking scalps,
he said, his voice too calm,
too measured, as if his keepsake

had my approval. The whores of Bangkok
were waiting, and there was nothing
to set us apart in their eyes.

It's Rock Man, a former Mounty.
Every day he filled his duffel bag
with rocks and carried them
bareback. The sun pressed down
on him like a hot iron.
Grunts, the real ones, passed by
staring. Before his seizure,
I taunted him with anti-war songs.
When he fell, I put a stick
between his teeth. Like the newly
dead, he did not blink.

4

In the red light something enters
and departs, maybe the moving
shadow of an insect. How careless
to forget where I am. Vietcong
tunnel here, farmers by day
who stalk the night. They pop up
anywhere.

I grip my stone, the only one
I hold onto except in a nightmare
where an ant makes me lug rocks
through a tunnel until I scream.
I swear, there are fissures
in my forehead no one sees.

I'm no better than a bug—squeezed
into a carapace that I've
outgrown, ready to molt. Except
for fear, I could jettison my helmet,
flak jacket and bandolier,
like the time I released a firefly
to a swarm of stars blinking
in an open field, the real ones
shining above, light upon light.

5

War Dog guides me.
Rifle cocked, I stifle a cough.
Each step, soft as an ant's,
takes us into a field of stars.

Rachel Kann
free, fall

pluck the irises
from my eyes

the bloom
from my cheeks

dislodge tongue
from jaw
like the errant strawberry
it yearns to be

when will
pearls all tumble?

when will
the taught tautness slack?

define:
crux?
nexus?

lie in wait under flaws
and rickety skeleton

lie in wait behind lush
and respiration

unfold crossed limbs
transcend the panic of open

pulse quicken then slow

trust beyond faith
to the flipside of
complacent

bravery
proves its
essential mettle when tested

and only in that moment

just like commitment
just like commitment

Joseph Karasek
Something About

my coughings
and her creepings about, her bent, labored walk

that slow shuffle from couch to toilet,

her patient word, a handy subterfuge for
getting on in the world.

Is it only patience then, that is real, the labored waiting
and so, is there no other room

that this is what we have and what we know and
somehow must be made sufficient.

Today asks me to walk
on the other side of her, the side unencumbered by a cane.

Waiting, distracted, I do not hear
the silvered bolt loosed from some bumper,

see its careful slide along her shoe.

In a moment she has already fallen.
It's nothing, nothing, she says as two men stop, help get her up.

Her purse lies open on the street.

Suddenly, I trust everyone..

Bridget Kelley-Lossada
Soon

I will have to unleash
your spirit

into the air

liberate this body
of its weight

reenter the after burn
of my own birth

fall into light

give name to myself
and your flesh

I am terrified.

Ron Koertge
Losing My Religion

At the Illinois State Fair, I was given five dollars
and allowed to roam the midway. I didn't want cotton
candy or a corn dog. I wasn't old enough for French Follies.

Then I saw a kid carrying a giant panda, a panda who
looked like a god other prizes might pray to.
Of course, I lost all my money and didn't win a thing.
Moping around, though, I saw the same kid slip
between tents, return the panda to a grizzled
carny, and get paid.

I was a sensitive child, the sort of little pantywaist
who might grow up to be a poet, so I burst into tears.
A policeman led me to the Pavilion of Lost children.
I cried loudest of all and refused the awful cookie.

By the time my parents found me, I was running a fever,
and my father drove home disgusted, getting a speeding
ticket which he blames me for to this very day.

Michael Kramer
La Cienega to the Southbound 10 Then Home

I

These diners waiting on valets for their Jaguar,
these summer blonders tonging salad after shopping,
these drivers steering traffic past slow lights' congestion,
all wait unafraid as each time, each life commencing,
all pass unaware of all these events so painful.

And I drive home past clubs now empty, doors just opened,
and people line the sidewalk to the canopied doors.
These tears that streak my face, the anguish in my wife's voice,
no stranger need share; these others do not know this,
our pain remains a private charge, our solitude.

Our car, the bubble of our car inoculates,
our sorrow speaks so eloquently around this silence,
our car that passes furniture set out on sidewalks,
as people cross, the lights return from red to green,
our car approaches onramp to this freeway, home.

II

This day the black thick headlines speak so many troubles:
"Israelis Open Fire in Jenin Killing Four,"
"Doctors Fight for Twins Independence,"
"'Awesome' Wildfire…Could Grow to 300,000 Acres,"
the stories' details do not explain this anguish.

A soldier's error on seeing Palestinians throng;
Maria de Jesus and Maria Theresa Quiej-
Alvarez, 11 months fused at their skulls;
the personal tragedy and public loss by fire;
these grasp the headlines, spill the ink and take the airtime.

One life courses the balance, and we know in that
great hospital others wait, a heart, a child with cancer;
we know that ours are not the only prayers ascending mountains,
ours not the only faith that waits for a private answer,
but our grief slowly drills where only prayer can fill.

III

While we sat waiting surgery, a woman reading
Russian (the backwards rho and other Greek letters)

walked up to answer the telephone, in her thick accent,
"Are any here for Ruth Devine?" No answer.
And she sat back and took her book again, the same page.

An intern in the cafeteria (she seems so young!)
had eaten and stayed, head on the table in her booth,
asleep. And we feel tired, and we feel pain, and yet
a doctor said to a sorrowful man, "This happens with
in vitro. Continue your attempts at pregnancy."

IV

"Blest be the tie that binds
Our hearts in Christian love.
The fellowship of kindred minds
Is like to that above.

"Before our Father's throne
We pour our ardent prayers.
Our fears, our hopes, our aims are one,
Our comforts and our cares.

"From sorrow, toil, and pain
And sin we shall be free,
And perfect love and friendship reign
Through all eternity."

V

So I, through these salt streaked glasses, watch
for the light to turn. Right turn on La Cienega.
I'll drive some miles, the stores will turn from affluence,
the lights will turn, and people walk or drive, and I'll
drive waiting for a sign, the Southbound 10, then home.

Judy Kronenfeld
This is not a religious poem

Lying belly-down
on the surgeon's table,
hands squirreled under my neck,
for a "minor excision"
of a "mildly suspicious"
protuberant nub on my back.
No-one's chatting. Especially
because, it appears, the anaesthetic's
not yet working. The surgeon's getting annoyed,
the way surgeons do when your flesh
doesn't do what it's supposed to—
come out neatly, go numb—
and I feel he's about to put the blame
on me. Then the—scalpel—is it? OUCH
—just the idea of it—I'm about
to faint. "Just relax for me now."
Right. I'm grasping at anything,
anything at all and what pops in my head, Sweet Jesus,
is—Sweet Jesus—suffering on the cross.
A rootless cosmopolitan whose father
escaped the Nazis, now I *know*
I've read too much Christian poetry, too many sermons
in "Puritan Lit," and "Backgrounds of the Elizabethans,"
not to mention heard too much gospel music. I try
pushing him away, then making his feet swing
à la Monty Python, then I run through all the Hebrew
names of God—at this moment that feels
so extreme, I *need* to wave some true colors—
Adonai, Jahweh, alias *Jehovah.* But they mean nameless,
He Who Cannot Be Named. Cold comfort
to know how virtuous are those who shun graven images,
or who understand God is a principle—the incarnation
of the community maybe, like Durkheim says.
The community's not at home; or at least
not answering their doors. What I want
is an icon—fast. So, guiltily,
I think of him, ashen-grey, bleeding,
Catholic, no less, and now I'm sure
that even the frigging Puritans couldn't wipe out
the *picture* of suffering in the mind, whatever Calvin
said about God the Paw being figured as smoke, as cloud,
so we wouldn't *try* to see him as a person. Then the moment's
over; my idolatrous heart
leaps back into my chest.

Bruce Lader
Guadalupe Field Trip

for Robert Werling

I watch you move to the precise spot,
set up tripod, secure bellows camera,
fling the opaque hood over them
like a magician, step inside
the darkened cockpit, a pilot plotting trajectory,
stabilizing his craft. Surveying

Oceano dunes like a hovering condor,
you balance the composition,
frame the meandering trails
of snake, mole, raccoon, coyote:
letters flourished across a slope,
then pull from leather bag the yellow
filter to screen out glare,
meter for a millisecond exposure
of reflected sunlight, load a negative slide.

Everything in the window is textured contours
swelling to fishbone clouds in blue.
Holding the end of the cable release cord
connected to the art you depend on
for survival, a calm in the wind,
click open the shutter.

On the horizon, the landing area is a chute
of night descending to infrared
developing room, galleries, museums,
studios of prints. Collectors of light
and shadow peruse your books,
travel with you around the world.

Viet Le
Asphalt Cocktail

(2 p.m., First Day of Spring in L.A.)

In this sunshine
even the scrawled stucco looks edible
like dyed script on a birthday cake.

Prisms reflect off glass and metal,
glacial storefronts.

Speeding on Santa Monica Boulevard
past the Sears that slow-burned
like a cigarette in the riots—
yes, this was the block
now baptized in a wash of light.

Ragtag hustlers in tank tops, denim
in front of Spike's bar
clucking like church hens.

Potholes and heat.

Glint of chrome tubing, dirty blonde, sidewalk:
a wheelchair-bound woman,
middle-aged
secretarial, pale and sagging
like a dough mound.

Stark against blank façade and pavement
in a thigh high
crushed velvet dress,
spaghetti straps and grocery-sack cleavage
zircon dewdrop necklace—

head back
eyes closed
arms outstretched
like Jesus in *The Last Supper*
legs spread
immobile
as if she was basking at the beach.

Carol Lem
Window Watching

Why do I keep returning
to this window: the shingled roofs
cracking under an August sun,

the old woman across the way,
pulling a thread through a worn sock,
the fern wilting on the balcony railing,
those hazy San Gabriel mountains—

my Shangrila mountains
as though out of reach,
a backdrop for the main stories:

her grandson who shoots out
from the gate swinging
a sword kung fu style, and she
saying something in Chinese
he ignores.

Each in their play, but when
dusk descends they go in together
and light the stove.

Little do they know
of the other story taking place
as she shuts the blinds
of their window facing mine,

the story of a woman
who watches a grandmother
mend sock after sock as though
they were heirlooms
and not off the rack at Kmart.

And what am I mending
word after word, a woman alone
with two cats and a laptop
tapping on lives
because I can't remember

a grandmother who died
before I was born, a grandson
who could have been my uncle
before the booze and blonds

and maybe had one moment
with socks and sword.

A moment not so out of reach
when words and the imagination
stride side by side,

when I too
can cross swords with an
ancestral story

where a grandmother
talks of her childhood in Xi-an
that I might ignore only to retell it
fifty years later,

her face still glowing
under the noonday sun.

Sylvia Levinson
Linkages

If the life and the soul are sacred, the human body is sacred
—Walt Whitman, *Leaves of Grass*

They always look so elegant,
those line drawings, black ink,
reds and golds in The Kama Sutra.
His turban never askew or unwound,
her sleek ebony hair, not one strand undone.
Their robes, discreetly pulled aside or
they are naked except for their sumptuous jewelry,
anklets, bracelets, ropes of emeralds, rubies,
pearls, draping their smooth, taut bodies.
Position flawless, they Ride the Tiger,
acrobatic joining of linga and yoni.

You and I, voluptuaries on rumpled sheets, sweat.
My mascara smears. Our ample flesh, all
moguls and crevices, freckled, dotted with moles.
The scent of the sea, bread rising, fills the room.
Our juices, thicker than tears, glisten on our thighs.
Inelegant and satisfied, regaining breath, we rest
in the classic pose: arms flung wide, your leg draped over mine.
The pulse behind your knee messages contentment.

Victoria Locke
Introduction to Entomology

In early spring
Ladybug's came to visit by the thousands
Feasted on aphids
I let the milk thistle
And mustard weeds grow chin high
Week after week I sent the gardener away
"The ladybugs are still here, come back next week"
By June they had disappeared and the weeds stood drying
Their helicopter seeds whirling off days before
And in their wake the
Black Widows arrived
A plentiful warning
They are bold
They are everywhere
In empty flower pots in full sun
Under the eves at my back door
Defying convention of low dark and moist
They inhabit the very places
They aren't supposed to like
They are defiant
They are everywhere
Red hourglass beauties
I understand the dangers of letting them live
The strange symmetry of their arrival
Parallels a dwindling ration of people
A lover's drought lasting years
Strange dust bowl of the season
I can feel the approaching summer
Dry in my bones

Gerald Locklin
vincent van gogh: *the mulberry tree,* 1889

in the artist's words,
"its dense yellow foliage
was of a magnificent yellow color
against a very blue sky,
in a white stony field
with sunshine from behind."

he neglected to mention that
he'd plugged the whole scene into
god's own infinitely voltaged battery.

no one was ever more alive than he.
it is not just that
he was creative:
he embodied creation…
the creator took possession of him.
death and life were one:
both crackled with brain-music.

he may have known something
that we do not, yet,
a reality defying words.

his brain exploded into galaxies.

Melisande Luna
A Paiute Woman's Dim Memory

Today I run my palms over ghosts,
let my fingers seek the cups
of *matate* hollows in the granite,

worn by fawn-fleshed girls
as they worked manzanita fruit
and pine nuts to paste between rocks.

No *manos* remain, only the mountain
to explain the methods of women gone to sinew and silt,
who came to grind their testimonies
in the memory of stone.

Rick Lupert
How Close Was Mars?

Mars was so close you could see it next
to the moon like they were conjoined.

So close I had to duck when walking up the stairs.
Mars was so close sixty-six thousand years of

history dropped in my late summer bucket like
Los Angeles rain. Mars knocked on my door

last night. Said, in a hurried fashion
"Get the hell out of my way." Mars

You're so close, the property values are changing.
You want a glass of water Mars? It's a trick

Question. The scientists made me ask it.
Mars, a seed fell off your surface and landed in

our atmosphere. A strange tree sprouted and
grew as tall as a dozen fire hydrants. Mars,

you were so close the new gravity uprooted
that tree and it fell back to you. We're building

a chunnel to you Mars. Will you visit? Would
you like some potato chips? Don't answer!

The knowledge would give us an unfair advantage.
Mars, I remember when you were a smidgen,

a twinkle, a bissel. A pinpoint of red, just left
of the moon. Just a pinch of you in the sky

giving confidence to the Hungarians. We clutch
our telescopes under our beds Mars

hoping you'll think we're not home. We're out
eating goulash, we're not worth coming so close.

Glenna Luschei
Time is the Canoe

This morning I woke up
as a scrub jay dove into wisteria.
I looked down when a loquat fruit
hit my foot.
Where did spring and this industry
come from?

I have been tracking the voluptuous
odor in the library stacks,
not the scent of magnolia in water.

This morning, I cracked open a Brazilian
story, "The Third Bank." A man
hacks out a canoe and paddles the river
forever, through his daughter's wedding,
his son's rite of passage.
What is the meaning of his canoe:
his sarcophagus? and for the third bank:
his heaven?

I know. Time is the passage of the canoe.
It's the same here.
We climb into our vehicles
leaving the ones who love us yearning.
We go on unswerving, not looking
left or right. We do what is to be done.

Sarah Maclay
Whore

It comes from *hore* in Old English,
hora in Old Norwegian,
but the Latin references charity—
at the root it's *carus*—dear,
as in *Hello, whore. Hello, dear.*
As in loved one, sweetheart, precious,
as in rare—therefore expensive, dear,
cher, cheri, a luxury
when given freely,
pitting charity against law.

Amy MacLennan
The Beauty Shop

Her name was Opal, and she did
my grandmother's hair,
or "fixed it" as Grandma said,
as if the task of combing
and cutting grey curls
took a bit of engineering,
a knack for making it right.
Every third Saturday
we went downtown,
the sweet sting of shampoo,
straightener, bleach
hitting us well before
we walked into the blast
of moist air and dryers,
Opal waving me to the magazines,
Grandma to the only empty basin.
Opal was all texture,
her face a relief of creases,
her frizzy mane pulled back
to a braided bun. She called
all her customers girls
(I was "young lady")
and they buzzed
about The Edge of Night,
Days of Our Lives, as she rolled
swatches of hair into curlers,
jabbed in bobby pins,
brushed off clippings.
Grandma napped as her hair dried,
and sometimes Opal stepped out
to smoke. Leaning against
the screendoor, she flicked ashes
from her Winston, drank coffee with cream
in a styrofoam cup. She rubbed
her wrists with ointment, took an aspirin
every time, and more women came in
for tints, sets, permanent waves,
paid Opal with cash,
placed their hair
in her knotted hands.

Melanie Martin
Poem for Singer

On my lap is what will be
your book come September,
month of crepe myrtles and sweet olive.

My birth in August brought water lilies,
kangaroo paws, bottle trees, ginger,
delavay magnolias, daylilies and oleanders.

Five years earlier, in December,
your mother's belly was swollen & full
and the garden was thick & wide with holly
and Himalayan cherry, aloe, Australian Cassia,
Japanese apricots, Iceland poppies and floss silk trees.

This March, we window-shopped,
carved, crystal chandeliers
and canopy beds behind glass.
Magenta azaleas and Australian mint
bloomed while our hands were palm to palm.

Holaday Mason
Memorial Day In L.A.

We drove all over town today, searching
for a new mattress, a commitment of depth.
Tied to the roof of the truck, at every red light,
the Serta Perfect Sleeper stopped
flapping the wings of its plastic sheath,
and the pressure of silence filled up the space.

Our old mattress was king size.
When I stripped it of sheets, you noticed
an almost perfectly round yellow stain,
big as a head or the expanse of a woman's hips,
and you ask me where it came from.
The bed had belonged to Merrill,
who'd died so badly on the 101 freeway
that her husband could not retrieve her
handbag, her day things, from the ruined Toyota.
Should have bought new tires. Should have
called her home for dinner. Should have
moved to Japan. His best friend, Henry,
braved the dire task, then whispered for months
about the bits of skin, smears, spatters
and everywhere threads of her long red hair.

I tell you the mark may have come from her:
leftover chromosomes, chemicals, nocturnal flooding,
the lasting color of her menstrual blood,
her vomit, a bad night sweat or a piece
of the marriage. One simple blotch,
at the head of the bed or under the pelvis, where once
she'd had a vagina. Or it could have just been
a glass of wine spilled at a party.

Now across the brand new mattress, my legs
lie still in pajamas shiny with age.
Feet, bland sheep follow along wherever I go.
Clean white cotton conforms to the privacy of my skin.
Padded, this bed is patient with my captivity
my body, this cage of soul from which I listen as
the late local news informs the whole world,
"Science has discovered the best cure for winter
blues is a lot of bright white light."
Well we have that here. Everywhere.

Ellyn Maybe
Postmedieval Mozart

His hands were made of pinwheels as he slid them down the piano,
like the keys would open rooms full of illuminated manuscripts
and black velvet Jerry Lewis museums.

There were watercolors in my eyes, this holy dance when one sees someone
doing the thing they were put on Earth to do.

Language beyond words.
Sound beyond vibration.

He laid his head on the piano like a time in history
before anyone had a notion of guillotine.

Suddenly, he'd stand, punching a hole in the musical ozone layer
with his buoyancy.

The sweat ate his face like a pearl that sits on the tongue
of an oyster's drama.

If Dali wrote songs, they would've shared charts.

This outside music - outside of radio - outside of cookie cutter dough.

Hitchcock movies roll off the cliff of my mind in the suspense
of your octaves.

There's a candelabra you're lighting in my throat.

There's a child playing chopsticks at a 24 hour Chinese restaurant
with a lounge and 15 card decks.

There's a hush in my lips as I shush the room conditioned
by a millennium of mediocrity to talk through greatness.

You come like an ice cream truck for the misfits
with cathartic custard and bonfire bonbons.

There is a Casablanca in your keyboard.

There I am with my wood
building a pedestal.

This world has never fully understood the dissonant, or the dissident.

Michael McClintock
Raspados

The hour when the horned dog sleeps, that hour,
And the moon's a pale, humid smear in the sky
Over the freeway, the electric plant, the brewery,
The blocks of warehouses, that moon
At the end of the long avenue, suspended
Above the trees and small homes and apartments

And the evening air's a moist breath of voices, those voices
At the end of all the long avenues, our voices

Tired in the dark, the languid hour after dinner,
Tired from the world's canning, the world's stitching machines,
The lathes and hot lights and liquid metals,
The smell of grease and ozone, cement and tar,
Deaf from the buzzing saws,
Deaf from the hammering presses,
Deaf from drills endlessly drilling, ceaselessly
Laboring for that foot in the ass—

There is an old man from Calexico,
A man mute and blind in one eye,
Who comes along pushing a small cart
Carrying rainbows of color on shaved ice,
Syrups of orange and yellow and green,
Cool fantasies in sugar for a dollar.

We listen for him, his sound
The dreamy tinkling of tin bells
Coming out of the purple splash
Of tree-shadow—our eyes on him,
Finding him, the only man in the world
Good for the eyes at that hour—that man
Selling syrups on sparkled ice, bringing to us
Sweet, cooling, tasty raspados.

Daniel McGinn
The Structure of Language

1. (a found poem, from the introduction to the textbook " The Structure of Language,"
   page 16)

Consider the following utterances, all of which are odd for different reasons:

(1) I just swallowed my nose.
(2) I will show you fear in a handful of dust.
(3) This lovely red rose is a red rose.
(4) Physical objects do not exist.
(5) I have just been decapitated.
(6) Pain is the stimulation of C-fibers

Thus, accused of having used language oddly, the metaphysician who replies
"So what?" replies correctly.

2. So what?

So what is the correct reply?

Sorrow exists as sure as children play. Pain is
The stimulation of c-fibers.
There is magic in the air. Pain is hope sneaking out the back door.
Objects that don't exist break bones in your body.
Pain wakes up next to you like smallpox
Crying in a blanket.

I have not swallowed my head
I have just been decapitated.
It could have been worse.
I might have been castrated.

At first I was afraid that you were ignoring me
But now I realize that you are not really there
And I am not really here. So what
You reject is the illusion. And I thought it was me.
It's not that you don't see me but I've been talking
to a ghost. Clear as the chair I'm not sitting on. Like
Myself, physical
Objects do not exist.

This lovely red rose
Is a red rose
That will live forever
Because I wrote it down

I will show you T.S. Elliot in a handful of dust
Death in a penis
Poison in the air

I am smart as a bomb
I am rain from a cloud.

I am your private blisters
and red ruby cheeks.

Perhaps you have noticed that I speak with an accent
I come to you with post-nasal lips
Kiss me.
I have just swallowed my nose.
Can't you see the lump in my throat?

Lori McGinn
In Lawrence Welk World
Escondido, California

The pool is a womb—
a warm, gathering place
for old faces
worn out and smiling.

All the big dogs around here are
statuary stiff—
cold and toothless
standing guard.

They grin
at the Lawrence Welk old folk
who believe night will fall and
angels will come.

Old bones whisper down the streets
chanting their haunting requiem,
while grass reflects the green in God's eyes
hanging out in the land of mirrors
where even the bunnies smell death.

Joshua McKinney
In Earnest

Fall's gold is gone. The American
will reek another week or two
before the circling birds stop

dropping black along the river's edge
to feed upon the rotting fish.
One marks this season by the stench

of Kings—some picked to bones,
some bloated in the watery sun,
some carried home by fishermen.

A couple's Lab has slipped its leash;
it runs and will not be called back
until it rolls in what remains, to mask

its scent in throes of primal joy.
A pack of boys casts stones at one
that offers now as evidence

its last thrashing in the shallows
near the shore. I leave my footprints
with the rest. Along this edge

death is success; and its resolve to live
nowhere in earnest, now here in every
phase, is almost nothing, almost all.

Michael B. McMahon
Elkhorn Slough: Monterey Bay

Plowing through swells of night fog,
the restaurant at Elkhorn Slough rides
its pilings like a ghost ship.
Bluish light spills from the desk, profiles
a pelican—more shadow than matter—
roosting on a piling of its own.

On a rickety breezeway, I breathe salt air,
watch muffled lights of a barge below melt
into darkness deep as canyons that ballast
the bay. My party, just yards away, chats
inside at our window table.

We'd spend the afternoon in rented kayaks,
windmilling our way up the narrowing slough,
bucking an outgoing tide. Bug-eyed seals—
brown bobbers with whiskers—surfaced
about us, and fat sea otters lounging on their backs
cracked open clams with stone tools.

Amused by my airy perch, I call
to my crew, wave in clownish gestures,
but glass and mist double my remove.
they cannot see or hear me.

Arm lengths away, a foursome that glows
at my planet's core—daughter, wife,
life-long friend and his wife—
turning first towards one, then another:
smiles, nods, quick bursts of laughter.

Hovering out over water, on the dark side
of the window's glare, I can almost hear
them breathe, almost touch a hand,
and I suddenly know the flickering time
when presence and absence will be like this.

Drawn by songs and days of grief, I will be
close, although unseen. Then I'll remember
this night, say I have made such visits before…
then I'll remember the slough,
the foghorn out on the bay.

June Melby

Inside this circle

is an entire kingdom ruled by one

boy who named himself king when he was

five. No one knew how he had even learned the word

"king" but it was too late by then. The dog he named

"dog" and that was truly good, but the toads

he named "pudding" met a rather dreary end.

I will tell you the whole story one night

when we are draped around a campfire

and have already exhausted the supply

of non-toad stories.

Bill Mohr
Slow Shoes

Reluctantly she hurries, late
to work. Her ankles and knees
won't let her dash the last four blocks
to the bus-stop, but she spurts
a few steps anyway, to show herself
and the boss who doesn't suspect
her miscalculation yet, she wishes
she hadn't lingered in the shower's lush
porous whispering, sipped juice and coffee, scooped
sweet cantaloupe down to the rind, ironed
a kiss of memory with her blouse, wondered
about the daughter squirming at school,
and wavered on the phone with mother
who dragged her potted calla lilies deeper in the shade
of lemon trees. She slows down, certain the bus
will not be delayed, and if it hustles off
exactly when she would've sat, drenched
and panting, could she have lunged this final distance,
she'll stroll across the street, unfold
a newspaper, and ponder
who's selling shoes, the kind one can only walk in, slowly.

Carol Moldaw
64 Panoramic Way

Like easy conversation,
rambling, obliquely angled,
the winding street traverses
the steep residential hill.

Stone stairs ladder-stitch
the street's tiers; every few
rungs open on terraces,
windows glinting through hedges,

sunlight feathering grass.
At the first switchback,
pine needles tufted with dog fur
pad up the wide cracked steps

leading to a cottage and two
ramshackle shingle houses.
From the lintel of an illegal
basement apartment, magenta

fuchsia, silent bells,
bob and sag over a pot's rim.
Higher, up wooden stairs
built over rubble, we climb

to the top deck. What was
our garden now grows wild
onions' white flowers,
and butter-yellow weeds—

winter's mohair throw
draping a bare mattress.
By late spring someone else
or no one will be bending

to pick cool herbs
like single guitar notes.
Something knots in my throat.
Indecipherable

decibels begin jackhammering
inside #D—our old address.
Black Sabbath? Iron Maiden?
I know our own records

by the first chord. Pounding,
we try the unlocked door,
and pick our way through
a year's domestic fallout:

dropped clothes, album sleeves,
mattresses blocking entrances,
plates, cups, hangers, books.
I trip trying not to look.

Waving on the balcony,
an old guest, now our host,
offers us the view.
At this time of year,

no yellow beach roses
tumble the latticed railing,
no draft of honeysuckle,
no bees flitting near their hive.

Cars nose around the hairpin turn.
Looking past Berkeley's hazy
flat grids, past Oakland,
you can see, as if you've flicked

a painted fan open, a striped
spinnaker tacking the wide bay,
three bridges, and San Francisco
shrugging off her damp negligee.

Jim Natal
Filter

I wish I could explain how things
can change so quickly, a cloud engulfing
the sun and no logic of time or wind,
as when I was walking my dog
in the Santa Monica Mountains and met
the old couple also walking their dog
to the bench with the best view.

It's difficult to remember now the warp of trail,
the buzzing chaparral, the expanse of
visible ocean. I try not to focus on that one
moment when the man reached down
to pat his dog (a border collie, I think,
but I'm not sure) and his sleeve pulled back.

The Eucalyptus trees instantly changed
fragrance. Shaggy bundles of leaves
suffused with oily Australian spice suddenly
reeked of cat piss, then ignited into torches
(as the fire marshals always warned they could),
the canopy set aflame by those blue numbers
on his wrist exposed to daylight and air.

I don't know his story but I do. I have no idea
if Eucalyptus trees grow on brushy
Polish hillsides, but I don't think so.
I don't know how the couple found each other,
how they came to California (I didn't ask),
or how he can bear his dreams.

I only know that Eucalyptus trees
and chaparral, hikers and their dogs, can melt
and the background fade, the filter switched
so that only one color remains vivid and glows
as if the sun had turned into a black light,
as if a wrist had been dipped in radium and
that's all you can see when you startle awake
in the thick of some changing night.

Kristy Nielsen
Treasures of the Czars

To the hungry soul, every bitter thing is sweet.
Proverbs 27:7

A twenty-pound golden key, a lock of hair
from Peter the Great; from Catherine, a tiny braid.
Even simple towels hang stiff with gold embroidery.
Every hand-painted Fabergé egg
imparts another gift. I learn

the significance of five towers, the weight
of three centuries, and the truth discovered
in an icon descended from heaven, untouched
by human hands: *Mercy.*

I stop to let the tour move on without me.
I am thinking of every bitter thing
I ever said to you and can't take back,
of how museums never show the part
we'd most like saved forever, that lonelier truth.
But then, a painted icon lost

to centuries of smoke from incense and candles; only
consecrated ornaments survive. On charcoal
velvet, a golden frame encrusted with malachite
and tourmaline, with sapphires, rubies, 400-carat topaz,
and hundreds of pearls. Adornments cover
all but places where the face and hands
of Virgin and Child should be. What's missing

remains more stunning than what endured.
All that's precious is there, except the face
and its expression, the hands and what they held.

Kim Noriega
Heaven, 1963

It's my favorite photo—
captioned, "Daddy and His Sweetheart."
It's in black and white,
it's before Pabst Blue Ribbon,
before his tongue became a knife
that made my mother bleed,
and before he blackened my eye
the time he thought I meant to end my life.

He's standing in our yard on Porter Road
beneath the old chestnut tree.
He's wearing sunglasses,
a light cotton shirt,
and a dreamy expression.

He's twenty-seven.
I'm two.
My hair, still baby curls,
is being tossed by a gentle breeze.
I'm fast asleep in his arms.

Judith S. Offer
Return to Country of Origin

(1) In Italy, the Mona Lisa Was Grinning

At the Louvre, the Mona Lisa wishes
She could raise her hand to be excused.
Bullet-proofed, she suffocates.
Away from her Italian *sole*, her radiance
Fades; she looks chunky, stolid.
She needs a stone wall to lean on,
A valley of vineyards and olive orchards
To look over, and a marble *catedrale* rising
Across the sun-soaked *piazza* behind her.

(2) Can You Believe They Brought It Here on Purpose?

We didn't need Bermuda grass
In the first place. The hills
Were green all year, and crawling
With elk, rabbit, bear, grasshoppers.
Let us pull up all the Bermuda grass.
Let us send it back to Bermuda.

(3) Hyphenated Americans

Is Parmesan still Parmesan if it's
Made in Wisconsin?
Is Champagne made in the Napa Valley
Champagne?

(4) There is a Simple Solution

These whiteskinned people
Have been nothing but trouble.
Everywhere they go, the earth bleeds,
Diseases rise from it,
And everybody wants what he doesn't have.
Send them all back,
And the forests will be pure,
The lakes will jump with trout,
And "gold" will be just the sun's color.
There will be no madness, want, or war.

(5) Please Include Instructions

When tomatoes were first brought
From Mexico to Italy,
They were thought to be poisonous.

(6) But There Are No Jobs Where I Live

Three ships: Stagnant and stinky,
Leaking and lurching. Chinese on the decks:
Crammed and cranky, bilious and battered,
Starved and suffocating. Downsized stevedores
On shore: bored and belligerent,
Hungry and homeless, depressed and dopey.

Twelve bells sound from the Mission,
Float through fog to the clean
White Coast Guard Cutter
Rocking calmly on the blue-green swells.

(7) Where Are the Jobs?

I live in Cleveland but my job went to Oaxaca.
The factory just up and closed its doors one day
And packed all them cutting shears and spools of thread
And bolts of denim into 'bout eight semis,
And rolled my paycheck, my insurance,
And my twenty-one years retirement down across the border.
Some church people went down to investigate,
Said them Mexican senoras takes home five dollars a day,
And they live in one-room places on mud flats,
Where their kids play alone all day with old tin cans.
Shucks, we made that company what it is,
With a lot of careful work, year after year,
And they don't give two twiddletwats.

(8) Believe Me

The hormones don't change the flavor.
Do you hear the cows complaining?
What's the *beouf*?

(9) Please Leave Your Culture Home

You cain't say we's unAmerican,
Cause my folks was here 'for yours was,
And 'sides, Jesus wan't no N'Orleans boy,
And you ain't trying to kick out His religion.
Just 'cause we's killin a few chickens:
Don't you know: ever' God wants blood.
Leas' this ain't the human kind!
Sides, these chickens gonna die for a good cause,
Which is more'n you can say for the ones
Bein' fried and et in some houses.

(10) It's a Borderline Situation

Texas was theirs first, anyway.
Spanish was spoken there before English,
And some of the families that speak it
Go back way before the Spanish.
In the back country, the illegals camp
Where their *abuelos* planted corn
Before someone erased a line on a map
And chased the Spanish language across the
Rio Grande. Now, if *el Rio* creeps north,
If *la gente* creep north, if *el idioma* creeps north,
Perhaps we should erase the line on the map.

(11) It's Your Duty: Cost, Plus.

If you don't buy these tee shirts
Children will starve in Taiwan.
The snakeskin used to make these shoes
Came from an endangered species in Costa Rica;
You can't just let them sit on a shelf!
Brazilian rain forest was burned for your hamburger.
Babies breathe smog in Nigeria to fill your gas tank.
On a tiny island off of Tahiti,
The only industry is this kiwi jam.
Enjoy! Enjoy!

(12) The Last Word

In about a hundred years,
You and I will both be back
In the same country of origin.

Jamie O'Halloran
Near Clear Creek

Last of the snow melts
down the mountains

into granite falls, where flowers,
so like bleeding hearts, rise

through fissures that are so common
here. When I see the blooms that later

I learn are not rare,
I think of Japanese lanterns first,

the bright paper-like blossoms
in the shape of squash.

The lilies curl hard open.
Their pistils straight to the heat.

Maureen Ellen O'Leary
In the Desert

Desert initiates,
We study Joshua Tree:
The sun-draped cholla with its silent l's
Breeding light on left and right.
The ocotillo, run up and down with sweet frills of green.
Someone said, "Stand still—I'll dress you up!"
And clothed the smooth bare stock in leaves,
Promised flowers months ahead.

But now it's winter
And spring a fact to come.
The high round-shouldered rocks,
Weather-honed into endless possibilities
Of human pairings or objects
Left behind in the city,
Echo the sometimes gold sometimes gray December sky.

Carefully, conscientiously, we read the lore provided
Cling to desert details
Like the drowning to splintered spars.
We need it now.
It is the end of the year.
It is three years short of the millenium.
(I will turn fifty then.)

It is important to remember the healing properties of the jojoba,
To note as we trek toward Skull Rock
That "mara" means a place
Of small springs and much grass
To distinguish between nolina and yucca
To heed the warnings against
The fluff appeal of the Teddy Bear cactus.
(Taking a photo, you lean into its sharp spines.)

"What is that called again?" I ask.
In the same gentle voice you used
When I first asked you
Anything, you answer:
"Bigelow cholla."

The name is gone again the next time it appears.
I try not to ask.
I breathe the creosite-tinted air
Point to misshapen Pinyon Pines

Study the brochures.
Nothing sticks to the thin bones of my brain.
I cannot hold anything in this desert space.

Not even you when you turn to me
On the stiff bed of that dry motel.
I think of long roads and stretches of time ahead
And the hundred more years looming
Bigger than all the boulders in Joshua Tree
Heavy, hanging
In the now leaden sky
Pressing toward disaster.

It is easier to look up close
Carefully, conscientiously.
To ask a name again
Recite it slowly
Under my breath
To take it in, hold it against me
The length of an inhale.

David Oliveira
Picnic in the City

for Richard Beban

Believing asphalt
as pastoral as blue meadow grasses,
I spread a blanket
between two painted white lines.
From a basket
I take out bread, wine, cheese,
then wait for you to descend,
hands full of fruit,
to my side.
Perhaps the faraway hum
is the rush of a stream
we failed to notice
in our thrill to cross
the edge of the parking lot—
this near silence,
only the moment
before the larks rise,
flight full of song,
above the Toyotas.
The tall distant silhouettes
are surely mountains
over which the legs of history
have walked us to this place,
over whose flat tops
the sun will hover,
red from fatigue,
when we lift a final glass
to toast our good luck
for this beautiful day.

Judith Pacht
Praise Small Things

Red clay tradebeads in a dreadlock braid,
the scent of earth-musk after rain,
a cicada chorale shrieking in the sun,
the summer's chalky grass, oak-black shade.
Praise the sticky pollen on the bee's
hind legs, the blossom's private parts, the fruit.
Praise long vowels: *masa* and *metate*,
smooth and *avocado, quesadilla.*

Praise Nomo backing first base on Beltre's throw,
Cohen reaching Ahmed, Ahmed reaching
words both used to know, speaking, speaking.
Praise the wild geese, rising slow,
circling after rain to taste the scent
of air, of earth, this earth.

Jaimes Palacio
Why She'll Never Call Back

The mice in the walls are talking
astral projection, claim she accidentally left
her body in another dimension where doors are hard
to come by and they don't take
Visa.

There is some bickering and unusual glances targeted
in your general direction. Something derogatory about your
awkward sense of humor, your affectation for dead
musicians, your odd collection of sleepless nights.

Mice can be vicious and inscrutable if they sense
they have the upper hand.

There is an underlying implication that you;
the incoherent builder of houses, the confused owner
of lost baggage, have simply expected too much.

But damn't it all! You just hate to take the word
of mice.

These mice specifically. Stealing cheese,
giving bogus stockmarket advice, setting you up
on blind dates with dyslexic, bi-polar, Cinderellas.

Filling your thoughts with salt and small midnight
whispers.

Sherman Pearl
Blackout

It went dark in the loft. My first wife and I
looked out at the powerless city
and knew that the outage had started with us—
our broken connections, our wasted energy.
It went dark
and the switches we flicked
clicked hollow as the footsteps we heard
fading down the corridor.
It went dark; the half-burned candles that once
lit up our love-making threw our shadows
against the wall, gave my wife's soft features
a terrified look. The phone
was out, too, except for some futile crackles;
and the radio clicked
but had no news or uplifting music for the crisis.
Walls melted into darkness
so we leaned on each other; there is comfort
in clinging to someone you can't quite see.
We asked each other why
but the cause was beyond us and it stayed dark
till dawn. I walked down the stairs
to the street,
to the bewildered city just awakening.
There were rumors of sabotage,
speculation that the grid had worn out,
predictions that juice would flow before nightfall.
I walked on feeling surges of hopefulness
from the sun, from the traffic
speeding back to normalcy. I rushed home
but when I got there
the stairway I wanted to climb would not go up.

Sherman Pearl
Shoe

I'd have trashed the shoe and forgotten it
but the dog fell in love.
He brings it to me for a tug-of-war
and we pull back and forth,
fingers and fangs holding onto the body
for possession. The seams grow wider,
the leather more tattered.

Only the dog wants it now
but he wants it so fiercely he rips the sole
from its stitches, the tongue
from the gaping mouth.
He shakes the shapeless lump back to life;
laces dance like crazed skeletons.
He chews on the worn-down heel,
licks the residue of the ground
I've walked. He burrows for the foot
that used to slide easily in
and wearily out. Traces of shine
peek through before the dust settles back.

The dog's resting now and the shoe
looks like the shoe in photos
of murders and bombings, the lonely one
lying in rubble, one of the victims;
yet somehow, oh miracle of the craftsman
who cobbled it into a masterpiece
and the clerk who praised it into a sale
and the dog who has stripped it to its essence,
the shoe holds, it endures.

Candace Pearson
Night & Day: What I Know About Love

1.

"Love has to stop somewhere short of suicide," Walter Huston says to Ruth Chatterton in *Dodsworth*, 1936, They're in a foyer of the cruise ship, if ships have foyers. They're about to sail back to America from Vienna, where Ruth, his wife of twenty-five years, has cheated on him for the second time, when she says, "You'll never stop loving me," he shouts his reply (*Suicide!*), bolts down the gangplank and returns to Mary Astor, a much nicer woman, waiting in Naples, with whom he will launch an airline to Samarkand.

2.

"A moonlit deck is a woman's boardroom," Barbara Stanwyck tells Henry Fonda, in *The Lady Eve*, 1941, when they meet on a cruise ship from South America to New York, thanks to Preston Sturges. Henry's an ale heir who's been in the Amazon, collecting snakes. Barbara's a card shark (with a heart of plantinum) working the cruise trade with her father. Henry wants to get married; she wants it, too, but cautions him that women are wiser in ways of love, not to get carried away by the sight of la luna on water.

3.

This is what I know about love: not everyone gets a first-class stateroom. Some people are thrown overboard before reaching land. Others work in the boiler room or wait on tables, hustling for tips. It's best to check your ticket before you board, ask to sit at the captain's table, get off at every port. Then you might be Ginger and Fred in *The Gay Divorcee*, 1934, who meet on a cruise ship and pitch woo along its gleaming deck: "Night and day, you are the one, only you and you alone, under the sun."

Sam Pereira
The Sparrows, Who Might Die

for Susan

She pointed things out: The anniversary
That should have come and gone with grace.
This was the beginning of another year.

He kept the bottles in closets for effect, covered
In a fine dust, reminiscent of the years on beaches lacking
Water. Today, he remembered struggles, would-be lapses

Over time, when she'd say things like:
Will these do instead? Can this weary girl
From the North offer warmth in the strongest proof

Possible? Would you sip *me* instead? And finally:
I promise to die each night in smiles, in the ways that you prefer.
She might have said such things, had it not been

For those small sparrows, who began flying near the window, Blocking everything in
view. At last report, he calls to her
Each night, as though it matters; as if wind might be his ink.

Next anniversary, he claims he'll kill her something—a bird, Perhaps—and hold it to the
glass, so they can both imagine songs. Outside, in that mad and sulfurous air, no one
watches,

As a small, gray bird takes soul and all to Cuba for its warmth,
And the aroma of fine Maduro leaf. In the spirit mist of islands, there
Seems to be a girl, believing she still hears faint song: Sparrow cry;

A man's palm pounding the tops of two rusted, hollow metal drums.

Robert Peters
Traipsing Through A Cemetery
Huntington Beach, CA

For Terry Lee & Paul Trachtenberg

The cemetery inters Roman Catholics.
On every visit we see new excavations
covered with blue tarpaulins, and rows

of abused green folding chairs waiting
for mourners, and a dais for the priest,
the anointed grief-man consigner of remains.

Walking on the grassy tussocks of graves
gives the sensation of floating, until you
hit a gopher hole. You hope the jolts

will improve your osteoarthritis.
Your muscles snap and feel sweet again.
Your neck and hips are supple.

We are insatiable readers & poets and
each morning before we grab coffee and read
the obits in the TIMES, lingering over

the famous ones, viz., Kate Hepburn's,
and Robert McCloskey's—he wrote the
child's classic Make Way for Ducklings,

we stand by our beds at 4 a.m. scanning our
t-shirt messages for ones best-suited to the day,
perturbed that our Birkenstock sandals are not

better marked. Here, though, walking among
the dewy graves, I am disappointed how
these folks died is never revealed. A phrase

or two: heart attack, murder, old age, suicide,
car wreck, was he smitten with cancers like
suet in a Christmas pudding? Did she drink lye?

You get my point: to humanize the chiseled name
and yet not reveal who were the assholes, and
who the saints. Headstones lacquered with lies!

Four modest graves are particularly sweet:
one is for a neighbor Josephine devoured
in her thirties by cancer, another is for

a woman who, in feathers played Betty
Boop, a third contains Baby Cacace, our
friend Terry's stillborn granddaughter.

A fourth is for Dorothy Peters, my mom's
namesake. Both were born in 1906. Mom
died in 1963, after visiting us in California.

Terry actually finds her stone *Terry Lee*.
snuggled at the base of a gnarled oak tree.
She says she's amused, and meditates.

I see Mom in her coffin with her gray hair
massed in tight curls she'd have despised—
as she would the rouge and horrid lipstick.

I brush her clammy cheek and place my hand
over her folded ones, which will shortly dissolve,
consigned in perpetuity beneath seven feet of

black Wisconsin loam, beside Dad's bones
and the County Welfare suit he was buried in.
The undertaker declared that he must wear shoes.
He'd need them for entering The Pearly Gates.

An oak drops acorns. Squirrels scamper.
My folks by now are drained of body liquor.
They now have nothing to share with one another.
And I, alas, am in California.

Carol Potter
What You Need to Know

Apparently, even the sky is suspect. One thin cloud
means the plates are moving. Molecules being
released into the air above an imperceptible crack.
And the hot wind blowing hard from the east.
Five days in a row of 90 degree weather
and the ground getting so dry there's nothing
to hold the plates together. Common fact.
It's the shriveling. It's the heat.
Maybe the waves pounding the shore. Too many
waves. Too many pelicans. It's the animals,
they say. You can tell when it is about to happen.
When the dogs start barking and whimpering.
Or is it the cats upstairs jumping
up and down, and yowling?
The fetus in somebody's belly rolling around in the wrong direction.
signaling to mother with its little feet pounding inside her—
watch out, you'd better run!
Watch the pets and the pregnant women.
Watch the mothers running.
Watch how the palm trees clatter in the hot wind.
Watch the hot wind. Watch the water in the water cooler.
When it starts to wobble, it's time to run.
Watch the 10 freeway jammed, pressure of the cars
in one place on the plate. Or is it all of us
out on the beach today flat on our backs.
It's that man leaning on his horn
at the corner of Rose and Ocean.
It's Ocean. It's Rose. It's that drunk
falling down; he's trying to get himself safely
to the corner. And the dog barking, but which dog
is the real dog to listen to? The pit bull or that little
white Scottie sitting on the baby swing
getting happily pushed back and forth?
I thought it was a little kid in a furry
snow suit in the top of the summer. It confused me.
Watch it. Watch that dog. Watch the sand
blowing too much in one place. When the gulls
lift up all at once. I'd like to know when
it's time to run please. Time to be jumping
under tables or should we head
for the doorways. Should we prop ourselves up
in the doorframe, but which doorframe, or should we just
run outside? When we run outside then, which
direction should we run in, and how long
should a person keep on running?

Padma Rubiales Rajaoui
Elegy for my Carassius Auratus, "Whitman"

The only fun I get is feeding the goldfish, and they only eat once a day.
—*Bette Davis*

You are the earliest domesticated fish!
You breed in captivity,
you have a modifiable social hierarchy
(you recognize me as chief),
you are unlikely to panic,
and you have a pleasant disposition.
You can survive brief periods of being iced over.

Why did you jump, oh Whitman,
my precious, my goldfish?
Was it because your love,
(the nameless orange and black one),
died and was tossed into the garbage?
After that, your world was flat,
and perhaps you simply fell off.

Did you get tired of swimming in circles
around the fake treasure box
plastic seaweed,
painted rocks?
Perhaps you dreamt of bigger bowls,
cool ponds,
rushing rivers?
Maybe somebody whispered
words you couldn't bear to hear,
(if fish have ears)
like *Asia*, or *wildness*.

Perhaps it was *Myxosoma Letospora Cerebralis* —
the Whirling Disease that got you down.
Your brain whirling out of control,
spinning through jungles of plastic plants,
Who was to say which way was up?

As you lie dying on the kitchen floor,
If I had put my ear to your tiny mouth,
what would you have said?
I'm looking for that eternal sea?
Or perhaps, *Please, put me back in the bowl!*

Aaron J. Roberts
Teapot

for Stella

The teapot reminds me of her smile:
charming, floral, and altogether English.

Food was a way to show her love.
Hugs became briskets,
kisses became cookies,
I love you became, "have some more."

My favorites were the Yorkshire pudding,
bagels, lox, and matzo ball soup.
I remember my hands,
stained purple from picking blackberries.

Her face was a blue silk scarf,
a photograph of smoke-covered ocean treasures,
aged like dust,
intricate as the dawn.

Robert Roden
In My Flight from Sacramento to Orange County

Moving through airport security checkpoints,
I am routinely stopped, even
After dropping my shoes, belt, watch,
Wallet, change, keys and pens
Into the institutional-gray collection tray.

With my pants hanging half off my butt
(At last, I'm in style)
I pass through the clanging gate,
Wondering if Cerberus or St. Peter will
Greet me, but I get: *male assist on one.*

It's the aluminum bracelet I found
In the street one night, bouncing
Across the asphalt
As I stood alarmed at the sound
Of dancing metal light in the air,
That gets me noticed. I always feel

Like the perpetrator of some crime,
Special, guilty of walking late at night
And finding treasure in the avenue.
I refuse to remove the band from my wrist,
So the hulking TSA man looms to scan me.

Lots of Indian guys wear those, he says,
Raising the black bar, *But that's their religion.*
You just wear it 'cuz you're pimpin,
Ain't 'ya? he nods, grazing the rivets
Of my sagging jeans as his magic wand
Emits two short beeps.

That's right, I say, glad to be recognized
As the prodigal O.G. returning to O.C.
Ascending with a ringing in my ears.

Zack Rogow
Flight 000

is the queasiness

when you're about to land

and you realize that this flight

with its snow mountain geodes

and its looking-glass lakes

this flight

which could have taken you anywhere

is actually going to drum down

in one certain city

where cars ghost along the artery

and families with wounded microwaves

and actual names sleep

in those dollhouses beyond the runway

and your life is not all lives

but only the best one

you can reach

Danny Romero
"Riots"

My mother can't stop crying
On the phone she says
She wasn't scared
In '75 because she guesses
My father was alive
And we were all together
—a family—5 boys, 2 girls
All nine of us in that same house
2 bedrooms, 1 upstairs, 1 down
A dining room for sleeping space
A living room, an attic
2 toilets, 1 bathtub
A garage and trees in a big yard
Near Roosevelt Park
In a barrio called Florencia 13
South Los Angeles
With a gun.

Lee Rossi
Eclipse

After the fourth course and fifth bottle of wine
we wife, my friends, and I stumbled onto
the porch, just in time to see Earth
takes its first bite of the moon's mottled bleu.

Somebody said the moon always
reminded him of a guy with bad acne,
Tommy Lee Jones perhaps.
I said it reminded me of my boss,

the pocked inventor of the tetrahedral spike.
a clever little gadget
you could drop from an unseen B-52
into rice paddies miles below

and which always landed point up
ready to pierce boot, sandal, or naked foot.
My boss was proud to have served his country
in such a demonstrably harmful way.

I wondered if the moon was disappearing
in Vietnam as well. Total eclipses are local events
like divorces and heart attacks. Maybe
they were just having a chest cold over there.

That's when I mentioned the murdered woman.
She'd lived in the next apartment with her husband
or boyfriend, whatever he was. They were both refugees.
At night my wife & I would lie in bed and listen

to her body slam against our bedroom wall.
Next day she'd say they were discussing their future.
I heard my wife telling about the murder,
things police want to know:

Who gave him the gun. How he tracked her down.
Why we didn't report the beatings.
Not why it's easier to see the big picture:
millions of kilotons, millions of casualties.

Or why, when you're that close to suffering,
you often look away.
The dance of the planets continued
until the eclipse was full.

The darkened moon didn't look like cheese anymore
or someone's cratered face, but like an innocent rock
hurled from who knows what distance
at some unsuspecting target.

C. J. Sage
Managing Myth

From time to time the red-winged blackbirds tumble
on the rainy air just above the shopping center
parking lot. Turning the car wheels to just the right
angle at just the luckiest moment, braking often,
sometimes I think that mostly the small-and-fluttering
will survive, and the beautiful-through-darkness:
heart, flag, koan; elephant, embargo, ennui.

Now and then I like to think that thirty-some
years of grieving had an archetypal meaning,
as the Pleiades, lost forever running from a hunter,
are symbols of an innocence not quite forgotten.
How the girls scurried and scattered through the woods,
how they must have cried and beat their frail arms
and leaped into the trees, and from there....
The siblings disappeared almost completely,
became a dule of tiny flickers in the sky.

Watching for the errant red-wings, thinking of my own
heavy-headed past, I like to think that I am not
just a child of folklore and dark circumstance,
that there's a way to be smaller and still bright.

Mehnaz Sahibzada
A Sizzling Red Bell Pepper

Eating *flautas* in a Mexican restaurant
I think of the magic of food.

Tablespoons of salsa and fresh cilantro
remind me of my own native Pakistan,
and the taste of *samosas* dipped in sweet
chutney sauce.

My taste buds have visited more countries
than the rest of me, sampling restaurant
after restaurant in America.

I think of the first time an Anglo woman
walked into a Chinese restaurant, or the
first Palestinian in an Indian restaurant, or the
first Cuban in a French restaurant

and I think of the language of marinated chicken
or spiced salmon, and America's young history—bright
heads of lettuce poking out of brown soil.

I think of heavy hipped women running thick fingers
through old spices, and the mixture of tastes and skin colors.
Our sorrows and dreams stirred into every pot of rice
or meat ever consumed—every pot of vegetables.

Food is the oldest religion
most primary of mysteries
the mother of skin and
the father of myths.

Food—like life—a sizzling red bell pepper
in a large, empty skillet.

Dixie Salazar
Virgin Behind Security Bars

Only jasmine, chorizo and songs of suicide
sift through these locked bars
that would ruffle the wings
of a weaker saint. Still, I have no way
to leave or enter the night.
From my cage of netting and electric
lights, I watch the parade to Joy's
Liquor King, with elephants, angels,
aloe vera and America flags for comfort,
and black widow eggs rolled softly
into the nape of my neck.

Sometimes a falling star twines
with a cry from childhood, circling
back to its beginning; a song
escapes from a cracked headstone
and finds me standing here, stalled
like a broken down circus
on the freeway. But sometimes objects
that may appear smaller in side view
mirrors, really are smaller
and swerve into the moon's blind spot—
saving a family of six;
sometimes a bomb doesn't go off,
a cancer cell refuses
to divide, and someone
opens the tracks of their arms—
palms upward to the Milky Way.

These are the miracles no one sees,
immovable objects that collide—
the moon growling at a three legged dog,
the wind gathering petitions—and songs,
even of the faithless, who don't ask
favors, don't ask
if I can grace their dashboards
or tilt their wheels into the spin
when it comes, which is the real test
the only one
that matters.

Cathie Sandstrom Smith
If I Am Vincent

You'll never see me look at you straight on.
My eyes can't even agree on a plane, a shape,
I am primed to bolt at the first sign
that this will not go well.
                              The straw hat lies:
meant to ward off sun and madness, see how
the brim rotates, concentric arcs of color—
star tracks across a daytime sky, unpinnable,
spinning, while the shirt washes away
without detail, a convenient place to park
blue.
                              The background: a joke.
You might think this self-portrait is cohesive against
a broken and abstracted field of unrelated color. Look
again.
        See how the flecks of red shrink from the hat's
edge. I am the fragment—dropped into a carefully
planned and woven landscape—
                                        painted
to remember myself whole.
                              But who cares
about the body anyway? Two of everything as if
it knows its own destruction, carries its own spare parts.

Always a chance the canvas will riot:
                                        yellow-gold-orange
of this straw boater might break its sweat-stained band, struggle
        free;
                erupt into sunflowers.

I don't know what to send next.
                Perhaps a hand,
                                an eye.

Anne Silver
To Begin Again

Walking on the beach,
my hand visors my eyes,
and I notice the horizon
is not sky or water, just a thin
strip that brightens, dulls
then turns to twilight.
Do I too live between
two worlds?
The salt in the air reminds me
I am part of the sea.
The palm trees' silhouette
blacken against the sky
and I am reminded of family
who are not in this world any longer.
What happened in summer happened,
what didn't, didn't and once again,
the New Year arrives too soon.
I am not ready to return to the first page
with the turning of the moon.
Clouds are roiling from the south,
announcing the season of storms
to come. I turn toward the call,
the ram's horn as the ocean fills
each footprint, as if
I came from the sea
just a moment ago.

Joan Jobe Smith
Cauliflower

At the Farmers Market yesterday
amongst the leaves and grasses
of basil, cilantro, asparagus and
avocados, tomatoes, onions red
yellow and white, across from the
Latina woman in pink singing fiesta
and not far from the saxophonist
crooning Bird I saw the most
beautiful cauliflower I'd ever
seen: huge, the size of a Rabbit
Moon, needing two hands to hold it
two handsful of thirsty water but
we don't care much for the taste
of cauliflower so I didn't buy it
a bargain for two dollars and I
moved on to buy eggs and garlic
but later, I still thought about
that cauliflower, the bright dunes
and lacy crevices of it, how beautiful
in would look in a bowl like a bouquet
uneaten while it told our future
read our maps to the gold of our
souls but when I went back to buy it
it was gone, off to another family's
home to be steamed, eaten, add 20
years to their lives. And I suppose
it was good that I didn't buy the
cauliflower. I am too ordinary
for such power.

Barry Spacks
Dear Reader

I'd set out my days in dark words for you
but confession demands redemption, success
in the offing to carry us through, no sense
to embark without light in prospect (even
MOBY DICK was a great success
for the whale) – and wouldn't you rather have us
know *you* instead? your storied despairs
and triumphs (mainly how hard you tried
to triumph) along with some notes on the bastards
who did you wrong, plus the ones who failed
to do you, and how your step-dad washed
dirty words from your mouth with Palmolive (you still
can't bear the taste). So see my problem? –
the need for significant breakthrough leaves me
stuck as *your* reader, dear reader, wondering
why we need to learn quite so much
about your brutal first coupling, cramped
in the back of that smelly Dodge Dart, or how
your dancing gig at the Polska Club
turned crazily randy, not to mention
later ills and corruptions, the seamy
unbeautiful stuff that flesh is heir to,
no wonder we bury our mysteries,
leave truths unsung, except at times
in a whisper, maybe, pillow to pillow,
deep through the privacy of night.

Mike Sprake
Trade Winds

In my bathroom that harbors sailing ships
there is a mirror where asteroids of shaving soap
have ended their orbit.

Gazing at my stubble this morning,
I'm reminded of the de-forestation of the
ancient landscape of Europe razed with axes to build
shipping fleets for warfare and trade.
My industrious little fleet
has gathered for no apparent reason.

One ship made of cut horn,
the marrow long gone
has washed up on the vanity's Formica beach
next to the electric toothbrush—
the outboard of dental hygiene.
Despite the ebb and flow of daily rituals
her sails remain full billow
with a cargo of exfoliating soap in her hollow hull.

A Parisian street artist has rendered another ship
which is thumb tacked above the toilet.
With her bunting like sails
she suds on oily textures of auto paint
through a primitive landscape of smears and scratches,
and behind her in the airbrushed sky
two planets loom—perhaps
the source of this month's meteor shower.

On the ceiling, an embossed clipper ship
at the center of the Trade Winds fan cover.
The Santa Maria of my fleet
brings new worlds to me through cracks around the door
when she blusters through the windowless room.

Today I bathe in the aroma of roast lamb
and mint sauce mixed with the lather of lavender soap.
There are perhaps particles from Stonehenge,
dandruff off the shoulder of Billy Collins himself
and the ideas of mankind blowing in together
with the fluff from the carpet
and the hair off the cat.

And when I stand naked at the helm of the shower controls
behind the blue bubble curtain sail
in the hull of the porcelain tub
I can circumnavigate my own universe,
travel absolutely anyplace
where those inexhaustible trade winds blow.

David Starkey
Who Killed Chameleon?

Bart claims it was Brieanne,
the time she closed the cage door
on its tail. Brieanne says
Bart left the sunning lamp on
too long. Friends and family
are divided. Brieanne's kids
blame Bart, but they blame him
for everything. Bart's bud Ed
says, "How can a lizard live
without its tail?" Their counselor
tells them the issue isn't really
about Chameleon, it's about
their relationship, which needs
an overhaul. She tells Brie
to go home and journal
about her childhood; she wants
Bart to write a poem. Meanwhile,
the cage remains empty,
the couple uncertain
if they can handle
the responsibility of a new pet,
and Chameleon lies
moldering in the hardpan
of their San Diego backyard,
changing from green to brown.

Jeremy Stephens
shaka-buku[1] piñata

I remember how fun it all was:
Me, with the blindfold, twirling on a heel.
You, drizzled in some crepe paper dress,
   then hung up to dry...

but back to me,
   swinging poetry like a broadsword
   as if you were a piñata
   stuffed with epiphanies...

I wonder why
I'm left dizzy and disoriented,
   always last to the remnants of our verbal fiesta.
It must be you — or your scent —
   and I'm made slow and awkward in its embrace:
   so please,
   have a little patience with me.

I've just discovered the role I play:
   the surreptitious lover;
   the guy you see twice a week,
   though you're not quite dating —
   your battle-weary cuddle-buddy still swinging a pen,
   as if there were words I could write
   that would even make a dent.

[1] A swift spiritual kick to the head that alters your reality forever.

Judith Taylor
Accoutrements

after the female Surrealist painters

I am the little desk on which you carve your name. I am the leather boots in which you wriggle your toes. I am the blue chair you sit on when you sip your tea and think. The mirror you gaze into is my adoration. You wipe your mouth on me when you use a napkin. I am your bath water. Don't forget to clip your beard with me. The silk shirt you wear out to dinners? My skin.

My wit is the knife you cut your bread with. The lamp you read by is my insight. When you fall into your soft bed (me) your dream becomes my poem.

Susan Terris
Buddha is Floating on the Ocean

A trick of light and the white Buddha
from the beach house deck
shines through the window, weightless marble
poised on an incoming wave.
Beyond him, pelicans, a scribble of fog
across Duxbury Reef, and a mottled slice of
daytime moon.

This is a place of place. As Buddha sits
on a breaker, legs angled in a lotus,
so do I. As his hands rest,
the right on his knee, the left palm up,
so will mine. Our bodies have unlearned
laws of gravity and mastered levitation.
Our heads—fixed, top-knotted—
are only half-owned by their bodies.
Our faces,
distant now, cannot be fathomed.

Here as the moon draws us between its horns,
washes us with changing tides,
everything is old yet new.
Nothing hurts. Memory is sea foam
and flotsam. We love all yet none.
We do not blink, have no tears.
Our images stencil patterns over water,
glass, wave, and sky.
Tomorrow the sun and moon will appear again
with us or without.

Lynne Thompson
Scissors

There's no true synonym
for scissors. Everyone
with a Roget's knows that.
Rock. Paper. Scissors.
You can cut ribbons or cut
your hair or your toenails.
And by *cut*, of course,
you may mean *score, sever,*
abscind, dissect, disjoin, cleave
but scissors are instruments
unto themselves. Just like
you won't find a synonym
for Utah or any other State.
Oh, they have their flowers
and their mottoes although
when their names are called—
Missouri, for example, or
New Mexico—everyone
knows what's meant is a
money-grubbin' land deal
about boundaries. But many
things just can't be said any
other way: toothache, for
instance, or mercurochrome
or 1951. So, when I tell you
that *it's over*, I do not mean
to say *interlude* or *maybe*.

Carine Topal
Feet First

I was born
from the

biblical urge
to dance

barefoot
hobnob with the

old prophets
born in

intervals
tenderly turned

upside
down

refusing to
use

my feet
born loving

the ground
its contradictions

born with the
coming

of history
spun like

sugar from
the nightlife of

two refugees.

Ben Trigg
Alcatraz Looks Beautiful in the Distance

On the Golden Gate,
camera in hand,
I practice the only visual art I am capable of.

It is fall 2002, after the World Series,
and I am in a city
where the losers show more pride than the winners.
Steve disrupts this sense of,
"What part of losing don't you understand?"
by wearing his Angels jersey in enemy territory.
The honks of passing motorists express their appreciation.

Despite these car horn battlecries,
there is no enemy here,
only the team who went down when
the Angels finally got it right.
I begin to ponder the implications of the city that is home
beating the city that has always felt like home,
but decide some thoughts are best left incomplete.

My father doesn't understand
that though I care little for sports, and am happy that way,
the Angels' victory makes my world perfect.
He taught me well.

It is a year of impossible firsts:
baseball trophies and early love.
I am taking pictures of my best friend
wearing his arrogant glee and vindicated loyalty
as we stand on the symbol of the city.
This city tells me I am only different enough to be special,
and that ordinary is sometimes
a fresh from the dryer comforter.

The wind is blowing,
and it is almost cold enough for a jacket.
This is the best I will feel all day.

Duane Tucker
Gathering (for Bess' 98th)

The sky gathers up the dreams of the soil
and stones and tugs the forest from under his covers of mist.
Her doe-eye darkens. *There'll be no nonsense today.*
She dons her steely blue.

The stubbled fields meek as swept shag
gather themselves for another
day of staring stone-faced into that blue
hoping for a glimpse of heaven.

The sea gathers and leaps at their feet,
leaps and gathers the way our hearts do
with every fervid prayer and out
of a scrabble of low bushes

a swirl of birds, whistling
like a stream escaped its banks, gathered in again,
wet and shining by the Mother's oh-so-tender
hands the way you gathered up your

"little bit of heaven" every summer noon
and toddled her down to the flowers and the fossils
and the stories in the seashells that led her over
the stumble of years into my arms.

Kathleen Tyler
After the Feast, the Poison

A man fishes, back
toward the camera. His pole
slices the photo diagonally, two
triangles that meet in the dark
center. At home my father
cleans grouper pulling out yellow
guts and something red. We don't love
Christ here. He drinks as he cleans, glass
of bourbon half-moon
of spit floating across its amber
surface so beautiful. The hand that yanks
and tears is shapely—square
and strong—the blow when
it comes almost asked for. Lungs
caving, I pick myself up from linoleum
floor. Outside the kitchen door my
sister calls. It is dusk. A mosquito spray
truck begins its slow chuff past, high
whine of the machine sharpening
night air. My father drops the tail, head, eyes
glassy pink, into the scrap pail. We run—
my sister and I—in the wake of malathion
cloud billowing from the truck. Husks
of ladybugs, last week's kill, rise in a tide
of white, a ghost fleet we disappear into. Fog
shifts and a small hand lifts, fisted. My
sister gasps something I think *sprats* or *brat*
before her arm drops. Inside Daddy fries
grouper alone. Fumes mist
my lips. Someone has to atone.

Amy Uyematsu
A Ride Called X.S. Incorporated

Orlando, 2002

This is the land of Mickey, this sea of blond
hair, sunburned arms and strollers stuffed
with teddy bears, toddlers, six-ounce plastic
bottles of Disney-label wat158159he first of many
small robberies, each 2½ dollars' worth
to gratefully gulp as we wander for days
under a sweaty, spring Florida sky.

A haven from ticking bombs, this flight
into childhood is well worth the 50-buck ticket,
the 3-hour waits for 3-occasionally-thrilling
minutes of speedy twists and dives,
the long patient lines
for Goofy ears and Daisy key chains,
for Grumpy t-shirts, Pinocchio backpacks
pink see-through Cinderella slippers.

Even the most cynical among us succumb
where kids and capitalism can chime in
mutual delight to the marvel of Disney patents,
from pretzels and pajamas to mouse-shaped shrubs,
feeding a boundless appetite
from infancy to death.

The joke's on us as we ride into space
in the ship built by *X.S. Incorporated*,
so wanting to be scared by the imaginary
alien monster that we don't even get the pun—
the biggest, grown-up kids wishing the hardest
for happily ever after.

Fred Voss
93 Million Miles Close

It feels good
to sit at this machine as a shadow
of a smokestack on the roof of the factory next door
is cast by a sun
93 million miles away it feels good
as my machine runs
and the sun that there was 3 billion years ago
makes shadows
of each fold of the curtains in the window
of a truckdriver from Florida
in a hotel room a block away
What I do makes steel you can hold in your hands
steel
that opens doors
lets
trains roll
hooks
beautiful women in sidecars to the sides
of motorcycles what I do
I do with my hands at this machine while the sun
makes love
to flowers
just like it did a billion years ago
Let others run the world
The sun and I
will shine and cut steel
and the shadows of church steeples and the wheels of streetcars
will be beautiful
because we have never told a single man on the face of this earth
what to do.

Charles Harper Webb
Mysteries

To lie in this exact bed in this very room,
rain plinking my roof's cedar keys.

To scan the room—think "closet," "heater,"
"dirty sock," and tell the difference.

To watch sunrise silver one strip of my rug,
the rest left pre-Genesis black.

To picture the terrarium where gopher
tortoises rattle their cracked food-plate

and, for all I know, create the world
my jelly-eyes perceive. To lift

my hand and obliterate my bookcase,
which is an enchanted tree.

To feel the warmth inside my bed,
as if my comforter is a blue sun. To see

my shirt on a doorknob, empty of me.
To sense, under cover of skin, the body

I call *mine* pulsing and bubbling,
its battery good for just so many beats—

the sum total of fish I'll catch, and breasts
I'll kiss ticking away—even my thoughts

growing turgid as blood in a clogged vein
until one day I gasp, amazed.

Charles Harper Webb
The Animals Are Leaving

One by one, like guests at a late party,
They shake our hands and step into the dark:
Arabian ostrich; Long-eared kit fox; Mysterious starling.

One by one, like sheep counted to close our eyes,
They leap the fence and disappear into the woods:
Atlas bear; Passenger pigeon; North Island laughing owl;
Great auk; Dodo; Eastern wapiti; Badlands bighorn sheep.

One by one, like grade school friends,
They move away and fade out of our memory:
Portuguese ibex; Blue buck; Auroch; Oregon bison;
Spanish imperial eagle; Japanese wolf; Hawksbill
Sea turtle; Cape lion; Heath hen; Raiatea thrush.

One by one, like children at a fire drill, they march outside,
And keep marching, though teachers cry,
Through screaming and the stench of smoke, "Come back!"
Waved albatross; White-bearded spider monkey;
Pygmy chimpanzee; Australian night parrot;
Turquoise parakeet; Indian cheetah; Korean tiger;
Eastern harbor seal; Ceylon elephant; Great Indian rhinoceros.

One by one, like actors after a play that ran for years
And wowed the world, they link their hands and bow
Before the curtain falls.

Florence Weinberger
Stanley Kunitz in His Rose Garden

He was so old, I wanted to read his collected poems
backwards so I'd know, from the poem on the very last page,
the heart can grow wiser in the oldest body.

It was a foolish impulse; his life was his, not mine.
I had seen him on TV, already ninety,
tending his roses with an equanimity
that seemed to turn its back
on his century's lack of grace.

I think of my roses, which I leave in the hands of Ludi,
who claims to love them,
and lets them get chewed up by bugs
he can't name or kill, and I complain,
but now and then a few emerge perfected in their unfolding,
ragged petals waving in the midwife wind,
and I cut them myself, without knowing where
to make a proper cut,
yet each blown bud becomes accomplice
in a motley bouquet,
colors clamoring against each other,
their scent restorative.
The lesson I hoped to learn from Kunitz?
What makes the engine go? he wrote.
Desire, desire, desire.
How to stretch the years
when the days go so quickly.

Jan Wesley
Caretakers

Weather is setting up, driving
the birds crazy. I ask
what he is thinking. *They don't act like us,*
he says. *They are single-minded*
                             and anarchistic.

He pads across a Pakistani rug, slips
outside with a can of seed and twelve
birds swarm the feeder. Bees
on honey, light on hills, it's what they do.

Later he will lock himself in and return
to designs of robotic arms, thinking,
blueprints are lovely like lace, his life
intricately patterned, and rooted in math.

Beyond the first swath of hills
are diminishing orange groves,
where we returned after Anna's
death, where urban synergy is making him
                             think of peace,

where he will retire and the two of us
will live it out. I lean into his line
of sight and tap my watch. He puts his
glasses on, looks across a valley of barely

kissing buildings and a freeway
heading south. We look thirty again—
that year I painted life one canvas
at a time with him pumped up on physics,

and as it faded to dark, he'd come by
and we'd fly off in the MG, climbing
over misty avocado farms, riding
each other's tails, raising noisy Cain,
                             the works.

Leigh White
Send & Receive

I told you to go away.
What I really meant was
come closer.
I'm endlessly fascinated by the shape
of your nose.

I didn't reach for your hand.
What I really wanted was
for you to grab mine,
and guard it with your life.

We have never watched a sunset together.
I wanted you to be excited to see me,
even if it wasn't true. Even if you
had to force yourself.

A lie like that
would keep me coming back
for more.

Katherine Williams
After Shadows and Silence

whose eyes are the first espresso after customs
whose hair is an eagle spiralling the updrafts
the one whose throat is Hennessy
whose forehead is the Pacific horizon at dawn
whose loins are stacks of lumber in winter
whose mouth is an oyster in its pearl jacket
the one whose back is *Guernica* as it hung in exile
whose mind is an advancing hurricane
whose fingertips are the marimbas of Veracruz
whose tongue is a robe of silk crêpe de chine
the one whose spleen is Paris
whose ears are shiitake mushrooms in hoisin sauce
whose breath is autumn in Appalachia
the crook of whose elbow is a cove of pretty fishes
the nape of whose neck is borzoi and she-wolf
whose toes are the Moonlight Sonata
whose chest is Vesuvio across the bay
whose shoulders are the rumor of armistice
whose gaze cascades the canyon between us
he the sound of whose voice is perdition

Joy Wilson
I Dream Often I'm Van Gogh's White Iris

I met my father for the first time last night. Silly, really, considering I knew my father years ago, although I don't remember him. He was wearing a baseball cap turned round on his head and was with a woman who had lost her poodle. I found the dog and returned it to her saying, "My name is Joyce." She shook my hand, then he shook it too.

I drove him to the airport and said, "It's not fair, really. Not just you, maybe not you at all, but everyone I love goes to the airport. That's why I'm crying, not over you." He didn't touch me. Opening the door he picked up a case—he was now wearing a suit and tasseled loafers. He said, "When I left that morning, you were crying. You told me to wear my seat belt."

Once, on a very long trip to New York, I stood in front of *Cypresses* and cried over the thickness of the paint. Not the thumbnail moon or the twisting brush-strokes, but the way the paint had been layered so deeply from madness and loneliness and over time had cracked.

I read somewhere the more you dream of an incident the less likely it means anything at all. Tomorrow, I'll hope for Van Gogh to return, to paint me into a hundred committed paintings, cover me over in shades of blue, green, and yellow.

Cecilia Woloch
Happy Birthday, Wherever You Are

These days, if I think of you at all, to tell the truth, I don't think too hard.

Sometimes I feel ashamed I ever loved you, sometimes proud. You were too young for me, years too young, but you looked like a toppled god in bed. *Perfectly made*, I'd think; *Michelangelo's David on his side.* I'd count each rib and wait for you to wake, to stir, to live.

In the beginning, the voices were whispers I half-believed I could kiss away. Later, I wanted to press my two palms hard against your ears. As if I could shut them out. Or make you stop listening, at least.

You'd talk to that goddess over breakfast, pointing to angels in the trees. And though I'd feed you and beg you to cling fast to the known world, you would not. You shrugged on your backpack and left, one ear cocked skyward as you went.

I dreamt of you sleeping on my lawn. I took down your photographs, at last.

And then, one day, you showed up at my front door, unannounced. Said you'd walked all the way into the desert and all the way back to the city again. You looked like hell. You smelled of sweat and dust, dry wind; you stank of sun. You laughed that crazy laugh. I gave you all the cash I had.

Wherever you are now, I give you back to them, your gods. To your demons and angels and saints. To the murmur of voices inside your head. I could have held you once, I thought, and stopped you listening—for what?

Listen: I wanted to live. I wanted the wreck of your mortal beauty in my bed to keep me young. I wasn't ready for all that sky. I'm still not ready. Happy birthday. May the birds at least be kind.

Gail Wronsky
Poem

(It's already the end of the month
and I haven't finished the essay on Larry Levis.)

My love affair with lilacs
uses up one more day at the desk.

A bush. The sprouting unerringly.

The dead face in the coffin (his? or that
gray-beard's)   not more elegant
than my own. Don't
you feel them, all the ghostly undulations
here? More lilacs would purify this room.

Unhaunt it. Eros could slip out on Psyche,
leaving her satin flanks still damp. Her sex
still edgy from its procreant engorgement.

The problem is that ghosts don't
palpitate. They linger in our caves; they

lick my ears. We go without a trace, is what
he keeps on trying to say to me.

Robert Wynne
Elegy at the End of the Millennium

I'm having a little trouble being loved.
Traffic lights ignore me.

Junk mail floods my box.
Answering machines hang up on me.

Psoriasis splits me into an open sore.
If the body is the house of the soul

then I'm condemned
to constant renovations.

I wear the best shoes, hang cool clothes
on my frame: jeans of every color,

the sharpest shirts money can buy.
I hide my sagging belly and timid skin

from the sun as if it were God's eye.
But I know He sees me at night

waking up every few hours
to make sure the clock is still counting time,

pressing my fingers to my chest
and feeling the blood quicken

without knowing why
the heart keeps having its way

with the body.
When I used to act, I loved stage directions

because they always told me
what to do with these empty hands.

Sometimes I sit on the landing
between my first and second floor

pretending I'm in purgatory,
asking myself

"Did you ever notice
the color of the sky on Thursdays?"

"Who did you love most, and why?
"Didn't you know that everyone dies alone?"

"After all you've been through,
aren't you the least bit hungry?"

Robert Wynne
Van Gogh's Mona Lisa

Her hair is the color of wet haystacks,
her lips so thick with red paint
she can't open her mouth.

It's not so much her slight smile
but those wild eyes, bright green and yellow,
that follow you into the next gallery.

What was she doing with her hands?
You can still feel them unfolding like a letter.
If she had a voice, it would be pale blue

and quiet as paper.

Brenda Yates
Formal Dance

My poem walked into the ballroom naked. Well,
nearly so. Free verse never wears panties; and her fairy
godmother, too busy to sew a dress, had driven by
and honked, tossing a bolt of cloth and pack of safety
pins onto the lawn, just as the sprinklers started up.

My poem had been meaning to trim down, tone up
slack nouns and passive verbs, but hadn't gotten around
to it. So when the bolt turned out to be just an end, she
was already bulging out between the pins of a too-small
garment that was shrinking. A vaguely familiar

free verse offered her some punch, a few extras
that further strained the material, but he, too, was
bursting at his seams and didn't notice. She recognized
some villanelles schmoozing, and sestinas engaged
in their usual intense conversation, so kept going,

past the pantoums with glazed eyes and haikus in dress
uniform, who gave her funny looks. Breeding shows;
the sonnets are too polite to stare. They are the real
aristocrats. In spite of families that have always
had remittance men, scandalous affairs, and syphilitic

uncles who bark at the chandeliers all through dinner,
they carry themselves with a casual elegance acquired
in their blood and this with or without finishing school
or study abroad. A sonnet bows, asks my poem to dance.
She has trouble keeping up with five such graceful

feet and even though she's practiced in front of a mirror
for weeks, she spondees when he iambs, trochees
when she should anapest, and trips on the final couplet
kick. He's smooth and helps her up, turning to gather
her shoes which flew off when she fell. She knows

he'll try to slip them back on, but her feet have swollen
beyond all recognition. She runs, awkwardly at first,
then remembers who she is: shape formed to need,
used but once. Still running, she strips, slender
now and gaining speed.

Kim Young
Hum

Mom waves goodbye from under her heavy purse, from under all her
usefulness and synthetic morphine.

Think of insects, mom, the simple eyes and antenna, the hard spiracles
of the abdomen. The lives of some insects are so short they last only one day.
Segmented creatures—
a well defined head and three pairs of legs.

Mom told me she wants to move her alcoholic brother out of his pick-up truck
somewhere along the border of Arizona
into her new upstairs spare bedroom. Life is painful she tells me.

Of course I know life is painful—
full of unfair hints and secrets. I began to think of people who eat raw
seeds and day-old bread. They inadvertently wander, wrapping around themselves
someone's lost clothing, pulling along bags and carts of yesterday's newspapers.
Mom wants to save them, too. I think they might be alright out there collecting all our
forgotten spangles.

Insects can eat fabric, opium, cork and tobacco. They keep
the plums and carrots clean and can live inside fields of clover and alfalfa.

I listen for their hum in the clover, mom,
for the dark blue shades of twilight, for truant schoolgirls
lighting their first cigarettes. Everyday there are shadows from other celestial bodies
passing over earth, there are female honeybees laying eggs,
there are unspent work furloughs and
silver fish hatching at the mouth of some cool river.

Rich Yurman
Waiting for the Light

We want rings, sure knowledge, safety.
What we get is each other: night houses,
boxes full of mystery, apples waiting for the light.
—Lisa Lorea

You ate the apple and left me
the core. This is not some big metaphor
for our marriage, it's what you did
that sunny late spring afternoon
30 years ago when my cousin
Darlene stopped by with her kids
to drop off a card and a hard sweet
apple from her backyard for
my birthday. You two were already
well on the way to becoming fast
friends by then, so you piled our daughter
and her two into her car and drove
off to the beach, but before you went
you ate the apple and placed what was left
alongside the tiny star-shaped
card on my desk where I found them
when I got home from work hours later—
no explanation, no note, just the card
and the remains of an apple.
By the time the five of you
came boiling up the front steps
flushed and noisy, I was sitting out
on the deck sipping a vodka and tonic
watching the sun drop into the Bay.
That afternoon alone, quietly
celebrating my birthday, not knowing
where you'd gone or when you'd
return, was one of my sweetest
times in all our years together.

BLUE ARC WEST

CONTRIBUTORS

biographies

NEIL AITKEN is originally from Canada, but has lived in southern California for the past six years. His poetry has appeared in several print and online journals including *Diagram, RHINO,* and *Washington Square Review.* He presently serves as the editor of *Boxcar Poetry Review.*

WILLIAM ARCHILA completed his MFA from the University of Oregon. His poems have appeared in *Rattle, Drumvoices Revue* and the anthology *Another City: Writing from Los Angeles* by City Lights Books.

CAROL W. BACHOFNER is a candidate for the MFA in Writing from Vermont College. Her poetry has appeared in numerous journals, including *The Cream City Review, The Comstock Review,* and *Prairie Schooner.* She edits the online literary journal, *Pulse.*

JOAN E. BAUER grew up in Los Angeles. Her poems have appeared in *The Comstock Review, 5 AM, Poet Lore, Spillway, Quarterly West* and other journals. She co-edited *Only the Sea Keeps: Poetry of the Tsunami* (Bayeux Arts, 2005).

RICHARD BEBAN is a Playa del Rey poet who recently received his MFA in Creative Writing from Antioch University, Los Angeles. His work has appeared in over 40 national journals, magazines, and online publications, as well as 15 national anthologies. He and his wife, Kaaren Kitchell, were two of the five poets who ran the Rose Café reading series in Venice for three years, and now host monthly workshops in their living room.

MARJORIE BECKER is a fifth generation Macon Georgia Jew trained in Spanish language and culture since childhood. A Yale-trained Latin American historian, her publications include *Setting the Virgin on Fire, Body Bach,* and *Talking Back to Frida.*

LORY BEDIKIAN received her MFA in Poetry at the University of Oregon where she was awarded the Dan Kimble First Year Teaching Award for Poetry, and received her Bachelors in English, with an emphasis in Creative Writing, Poetry from UCLA. Her work has

appeared in *Westwind, Drumvoices Revue, Timberline, Harpur Palate and Crab Orchard Review.*

KEVEN BELLOWS is a Los Angeles poet who will publish her first chapbook this year. She is a professional writer and PR executive at a radio syndication company; married, with five children and seven grandchildren.

LAUREL ANN BOGEN is the author of several books of poetry and short fiction, the most recent of which is *Washing a Language,* published in 2004 by Red Hen Press. She is an instructor of poetry for the Writers' Program at UCLA Extension. Recent publications include work in *California Poetry from the Gold Rush to the Present; The Misread City; Gargoyle* and *Art/Life.*

DEBORAH EDLER BROWN was the 2005 recipient of *Kalliope's* Sue Saniel Elkind Poetry Prize. She is co-author of *Grandparents as Parents: A Survival Guide to Raising a Second Family* [Guilford Press, 1995]. She lives in Los Angeles, where she teaches creative writing.

DERRICK BROWN is a poet and singer/songwriter with duel citizenship in Long Beach, California and Nashville, Tennessee. Brown's 2nd place win at the 1998 U.S. Poetry Slam and 1st place win at the 2002 Munich Poetry Slam have garnered him an international reputation as a performance poet. His most recent collection of poetry is "Born in the Year of the Butterfly Knife."

LINDA BROWN is active in the San Diego poetry community where she taught poetry workshop classes for over twenty years. Her retrospective collection, *Journey with Beast: Poems 1972-2003* was published in Spring 2004 from La Jolla Poets Press.

MARK BRUCE works in Orange County for the Public Defender's Office handling major frauds cases. He has been published in journals such as *Rattle, Urban Spaghetti* and edits his own small poetry journal, *The Blue Mouse.* He lives in Cypress with his ten-year-old son, who is a remarkable soccer goaltender.

CHRISTOPHER BUCKLEY'S 14th book of poems, *And The Sea* has just been published by The Sheep Meadow Press, NY, 2006. Recently he has edited, *Homage to Vallejo* (Greenhouse Review Press, 2006) and, with Aledxander Long, *A Condition of the Spirit: The Life & Work of Larry Levis*, (Eastern Washington Univ. Press, 2004). He teaches in the creative writing dept at the University of California Riverside.

ELENA KARINA BYRNE is a teacher, editor and Literary Programs Director for the Ruskin Art Club. Her first book is *The Flammable Bird*, (Zoo Press); she has just completed *Masque* (forthcoming with Tupelo Press) and *Voyeur Hour*. Publications include *Best American Poetry 2005, Paris Review, Colorado Review, APR* and *Verse*.

MARY CAHILL is a native of Chicago, and relocated to Los Angeles in 1991. In addition to her chapbook, *Pieces of My Heart*, her work has been published in numerous anthologies, including *51%, Poetry is a Verb, Onyx Spoken Word, So Luminous the Wildflowers*, and *Runes*

R.G. CANTALUPO lives in the Malibu mountains. His work has been published widely in the United States, England and Canada. He is currently finishing a Ph. D in Interdisciplinary Studies.

JOHN CASEY works as an engineer for a defense contractor. Two of his poems appeared in last year's Tebot Bach anthology, *So Luminous The Wildflowers*. He lives in Redondo Beach.

CARLOTA CAULFIELD is the author of nine books of poetry, including *The Book of Giulio Camillo* (2003) and *Quincunce/Quincunx* (2004). In December 2002, she was awarded the first Hispanic-American poetry prize, "Dulce Maria Loynaz." Her work has appeared, among others, in *Haight Ashbury Literary Journal, Michigan Quarterly Review, Poetry San Francisco, Visions, Beacons, The Texas Review, Barcarola, Nómada, Aleph, AErea, Chasqui, Walrus, 580 Split, Sugar Mule, Caribe*, and *LiterateWorld*. Her work was included in *So Luminous the Wildflowers. An Anthology of California Poets*, published by Tebot Bach in 2003. She teaches at Mills College. Visit her webpage at http://www.intelinet.org/Caulfield.

Note about the translator: MARY G. BERG grew up in Colombia and Peru. She currently teaches in Harvard University's Extension program. She has written extensively about Latin American women writers, and has translated works by Angélica Gorodischer, Ana Maria Shúa, Clorinda Matto, Juana Manuela Gorriti, Marjorie Agosin, Laura Riesco y Carlota Caulfield. Her most recent translated book is Carlota Caulfield's *The Book of*

Giulio Camillo (a model for a theater of memory) published by InteliBooks.

JEANETTE CLOUGH is author of *Cantatas* (Tebot Bach Press, 2002). Her poetry appears in *Nimrod, Denver Quarterly, Ohio Review, Poetrybay, 51%* and other journals.

MARCIA COHEE is another MFA seeking gainful employment. She is the author of three books, *Sexual Terrain, Laguna Canyon Was Once a River* and *Bonfire*, as well as several chapbooks *Eurydice, The Dead, Improvised Night, Still Life, It's Hard to Leave the Night Alone* and half of *Cohcesion*. Her fourth book, *River* is ready for publication. At least she thinks it is.

WANDA COLEMAN is a Californian writer who has published 14 books of poetry and prose—recently, *Ostinato Vamps* (Pitts Poetry Series 2003). She resides in Los Angeles with her husband, poet and painter Austin Straus.

LARRY COLKER co-hosts the Redondo Poets weekly reading at Coffee Cartel in Redondo Beach, CA. His work has been anthologized in *So Luminous the Wildflowers and Beyond the Valley of the Contemporary Poets 2002 Anthology*.

BRENDAN CONSTANTINE'S poetry has been widely anthologized and he has toured extensively in the United States and Europe. In addition to leading advanced workshops for adults, Brendan also teaches poetry to teenagers at high schools throughout the Los Angeles area.

RACHEL DACUS is the author of *Earth Lessons* (Bellowing Ark Press). Her poetry and music CD, *A God You Can Dance*, was released in 2002. Her work has been anthologized in *Ravishing DisUnities: Real Ghazals in English* (Wesleyan University Press) and *The Best of Melic* (Melic Review).

RUTH DAIGON was founder and editor of POETS ON: for twenty years. She has been publishing poetry for thirty years, and her latest poetry collection. the last of seven so far, is "Handfuls of Time" (Small Poetry Press, Select Poets Series, 2002.)

J. P. DANCING BEAR'S poems have been in *Verse Daily, Atlanta Review, Seattle Review, Poetry International* and many others. He is editor of *the DMQ Review* and host of a weekly poetry program on KKUP. His books include *What Language* (2002) and *Billy Last Crow* (2004).

LORI DAVIS hosts the Gneiss Poetry Series in Palm Desert. She is a member of California Poets in the Schools and teaches poetry workshops in the Coachella Valley. Her work has recently appeared in the *Atlanta Review*, *Salt Hill* and *Hayden's Ferry Review*.

TOMÁS ESTEBAN DE SAN ANDREAS was a pseudonym of poet and translator Anatole Taràs Lubovich. Anatole was founder of the Not-Yet-Dead Poets Society in the San Francisco Bat Area and had work published in numerous journals and anthologies. Anatole passed away on November 16, 2005.

NITA DONOVAN is a former Los Angeles City teacher and is Alternate Facilitator of the Saturday poetry workshop at Beyond Baroque. Her chapbook, *I Didn't Want to Make Any Mistakes Either* was published by Spout Graphic Press.

DIANE DORMAN is a nurse, wife and mother of four. She has been reading her poetry on the local scene for twelve years. She has published two chapbooks and various feature stories and restaurant reviews in local papers.

ELLEN's two new books of poetry are *Reverse Kiss*, published by Main Street Rag, and *Gynecic Papers*, Conflux Press. She has had hundreds of poems published in journals across the country and in England. Her prizes include dA Center for the Arts, Blue Unicorn, Cape Cod Times and others.

CARRIE ETTER lived in Southern California from 1988 to 2001. She edited *Out Lout: The Monthly of Los Angeles Poetry Events* from 1988 to 1993 and received her BA from UCLA in 1995 and her MFA and PhD from UC Irvine in 1997 and 2003, respectively. Her poems have appeared in *The New Republic*, *Seneca Review*, *Poetry Review* and other journals in the UK and US.

MARCIA FALK is a poet, translator, and artist. Her books include *The Book of Blessings*, *The Song of Songs: Love Lyrics from the Bible*, and *The Spectacular Difference: Selected Poems of Zelda*. Her paintings can be viewed at www.marciafalk.com.

JAY FARBSTEIN was educated at UCLA, Harvard, and University College London where he earned a PhD. He began writing poetry in 1997 and has attended writers' workshops at The Frost Place and Squaw Valley; he works with David St. John and David Dodd Lee.

ANN FISHER-WIRTH is the author of *Blue Window* (Archer Books, 2003) and *The Trinket Poems* (Wind,

2003). She won a 2003 *Malahat Review* Long Poem Prize. She lived in California for over twenty years, and now teaches at the University of Mississippi. She spent last year on a Fulbright in Sweden.

MICHAEL C. FORD was born on the Illinois side of Lake Michigan. His debut spoken word recording, *Language Comando*, earned a Grammy nomination in 1986. His plays have been staged internationally and his book of selected poems, *Emergency Exits* was honored with a 1998 Pulitzer nomination.

AMÉLIE FRANK is the author of five collections of poetry and a spoken word CD. She divides her time between writing, music, hillbilly distractions, and her ongoing role as Poetry's Goodtime Gal, but only because the job of Sweetheart of the Rodeo was already taken.

ALBERT GARCIA's poetry has been published in journals across the country including *Prairie Schooner*, *North American Review*, *Poetry East*, and *Mid-American Review*. Copper Beech Press published his book, *Rainshadow*, in 1996. He lives in Wilton, California, and teaches at Sacramento City College.

RICHARD GARCIA is the author of *Rancho Notorious*, BOA Editions. He teaches in the low residency MFA in Creative Writing Program at Antioch University, and at the Idyllwild Summer Poetry Festival.

JOHN GARDINER co-hosts a poetry reading in Laguna Beach which is now in it's 7th year. He teaches English as a second language for an international language institute. Gardiner is a 5th generation Californian.

KATYA GIRITSKY has been writing poetry since she was very young. Recently retired after almost 30 years with the Orange County Public Defender's Office, she now makes her home in Seattle, WA. Her latest book *Hungry Women* is available through Tebot Bach Press. TERRY GODBEY's poetry has been published in *CALYX Journal*, *Rosebud*, *Spillway*, *Pearl*, *Slipstream* and others. A former California girl, she now lives in Maitland, Fla., with her husband and 9-year-old son. She is a copy editor at the *Orlando Sentinel*.

JESSICA GOODHEART's poetry has appeared in *Salamander*, *Rattle*, *Cider Press Review*, *Free Lunch*, *Partisan Review*, *Solo* and is forthcoming in *Spillway*. She lives in Los Angeles.

S.A. GRIFFIN is a Vietnam era veteran of the USAF. He is a father, husband and human being. Author of

Unborn Again (Phony Lid Books, 2001), Carma Bum and co-editor of *The Outlaw Bible of American Poetry* (Thunder's Mouth Press, 1999). A crash vampire living in Los Angeles.

DINA HARDY is the author and illustrator of the book *Grocery Shopping with Roy Lichtenstein* (Spout Graphic Press.) Her work has appeared in a number of journals and anthologies. She has summated Mount Kilimanjaro and has ridden her motorcycle alone across the United States, though, currently she is living a life of little drama in Burbank, CA.

JOHN C. HARRELL's fascination for poetry began as a child after reading *Mother Goose*. John has published many poems about his travels and the world. He shares his life with his wife and two children.

JOHN HARRIS's manuscript *Climbing* was a finalist for the US Poetry Award judged by Muriel Rukeyser. He is co-founder of the Beyond Baroque Poetry Workshop.

BARBARA HAUK is a long-time resident of Huntington Beach. She is co-editor of *Pearl Magazine*, and her most recent book is Makars' Dozens with Robert Peters and Paul Trachtenberg.

SUSAN HECHT teaches a poetry class at Saddleback College and her poems appeared regularly in literary magazines before she took a hiatus to finish a novel.

JOY HAROLD HELSING's work has appeared in the *Aurorean, The Lyric, Lynx Eye, Tiger's Eye, Tundra, Möbius,* and various other publications. After many years in San Francisco she now lives in the Sierra Nevada foothills of Northern California.

MARVIN R. HIEMSTRA, a performance poet/humorist, has performed and published around the world. His new book, *French Kiss Destiny*, will appear in 2006. Marvin is editor of the *Bay Area Poets Seasonal Review.*
LARKIN HIGGINS lives in Los Angeles, teaches in Ventura County and has been published in *Genre, Blue Satellite, Saturday Afternoon Journal, Matchbook, Jitters: The Best of Southern California Coffee House Fiction & Poetry* and *So Luminous the Wildflowers.*

CHRISTINE HOLLAND grew up and still lives in California's Santa Clara Valley, where she watched bulldozers transform a fertile land of fruit orchards into high-tech Silicon Valley. Christine received an MFA from the Bennington College Writing Seminars in June 2003. Her poems have appeared in *Bellowing Ark, Blueline,* and *Downtown San Jose* Magazine.

NANCY HOM was born in Toisan, China in 1949 and moved to the United States at age 5. Widely known for her silkscreen artwork, she is also a writer, graphic designer and children's book illustrator. Her writing has been published in *Writings From the Long Table I and II* (Kearny Street Workshop 1999 and 2000), *Asian Americans: The Movement and The Moment* (UCLA Asian American Studies Center 2001), and *So Luminous the Wildflowers* (Tebot Bach 2003).

ANGELA HOWE teaches literature at Notre Dame de Namur University. She has been published in the *Comstock Review* and *African Voices*. She has been a featured reader at the Petaluma MindGrind Reading Series, The Waverly Writers in Palo Alto, and Il Piccolo Cafe in Burlingame. She lives in the Bay Area with her husband and her beautiful son Mason.

ROBIN D. HUDECHEK received her MFA in Creative Writing, Poetry at UCI and has published her work in a number of anthologies including: *Caliban, the Cream City Review, the Ear,* and *So Luminous the Wildflowers.* Currently, she is teaching writing courses at Irvine Valley College.

ELIZABETH IANNACI is a poet, actor and singer who has been a regular of the Los Angeles performance community for two decades. She is currently one of the directors of the *Valley Contemporary Poets,* and author of two books of poetry, *Passion's Casualties* and the soon-to-be released *Renoir's Daughter.*

THEA IBERALL is a poet, playwright, and scientist. She has a Master's Degree in Poetry (USC) and a Ph.D. in Computer Science (U Mass). Her work has been published in *Rattle, Spillway, The Southern California Anthology, Common Lives/Lesbian Lives, Peregrine XVI,* and *ONTHEBUS.*As a performance poet, Thea represented Los Angeles at the 1998 National Poetry Slam Competition, coming in third out of 45 cities.
ELIJAH IMLAY received an Honorable Mention for the 2002 Ann Stanford Poetry Prize. He was nominated for a Pushcart Prize in 1999 and received a fellowship from the City of Ventura, CA, to complete a chapbook based upon his experiences in the Vietnam War.

RACHEL KANN performs in venues like Disney Concert Hall, collaborates with music creators like DaKAh, leads workshops for disadvantaged youth, and won the L.A. Weekly Award. That being said, she works extra-hard to rock it on paper. *www.inspirachel.com*

JOSEPH KARASEK performed as an actor and violinist with *The Theater Within* in NYC. He has taught music on the primary and college levels and led study groups in Philosophy and on James Joyce's *Ulysses* at A.L.L. at Carnegie Mellon University. Actively writing poetry since 1997, he has been published in *The Pittsburgh Quarterly, Paper Street, Janus Head* and other journals.

BRIDGETT KELLEY-LOSSADA is assistant poetry editor for the online journal *Moondance*. She earned her MFA from Antioch University and has studied with Cecilia Woloch, Eloise Klein Healy and Russell Leong.

RON KOERTGE recently retired from teaching at the city college in Pasadena after having worked there for a thousand years. His latest book of poems is *GEROGRAPHY OF THE FOREHEAD* (University of Arkansas Press).

MICHAEL KRAMER, a high school English teacher for three decades, has had the good fortune to have his work widely published since college days. The creative works of which he is most proud, however, are his four children by his wife of almost 35 years, Rebecca.

JUDY KRONENFELD, who teaches in the Creative Writing Department at UC Riverside, is the author of a book and two chapbooks of poetry, the most recent being *Ghost Nurseries* (Finishing Line Press, 2005). Her poems have appeared in numerous journals and in a variety of anthologies. Her current poetry book manuscript, *Unmarked Border*, is available to an interested publisher.

BRUCE LADER lived in Goleta, California for six years and in Oregon and British Columbia. Recipient of an honorarium from the College of Creative Studies at the University of California-Santa Barbara, he is a former writer-in-residence at the Wurlitzer Colony. His poems have appeared in *The New York Quarterly, Poetry, Manzanita Quarterly, Fulcrum, Controlled Burn,* and *The Malahat Review,* among others.

VIET LE is an internationally exhibited interdisciplinary artist and a published creative and critical writer. He is the recipient of a 2003-4 Fine Arts Work Center residency fellowship and a 2002 PEN Center USA Emerging Voices fellowship. He is currently a Lecturer at UC Irvine.

CAROL LEM teaches creative writing and literature at East Los Angeles College. She has recently published poems in *The Chrysalis Reader, Red Rock Review,* and *Runes.* A reading of selected poems from her current book, *Shadow of the Plum,* may be heard on her CD, *Shadow of the Bamboo,* with music by Masakazu Yoshizawa. For more information contact her at clem64079@aol.com or visit her website, www.carollem.com.

SYLVIA LEVINSON lives in San Diego, where she has featured at Claire de Lune, D.G. Wills and Open Door Books. Publications include *Snowy Egret, City Works, The Writing Center* and *Magee Park Poets* anthologies. She is a Border Voices Project board member.

VICTORIA LOCKE is a Sign Language Interpreter living in Los Angeles. She appeared briefly in Paul Devlin's documentary—SlamNation. Her latest chapbook *The Woman With The Black Crayons* is available at victorialocke@yahoo.com

GERALD LOCKLIN's most recent book from Water Row Press is *The Pocket Book: A Novella and Nineteen Short Fictions,* 2003.

MELISANDE LUNA is a renegade geologist who raises parrots, orchids and eyebrows in Central California. Her poetry and essays have appeared in a variety of print and electronic publications including *The Edinburgh Geologist, Parrot Chronicles,* and *Voyages,* an anthology of world poetry.

RICK LUPERT has been involved with the Los Angeles Poetry community since 1990. He is the author of 9 books, most recently *Stolen Mummies: The Poet's Experience in London.* He created and maintains the *Poetry Super Highway,* a major online resource and publication for poets and writers, and has hosted the long running weekly Cobalt Café poetry reading in Canoga Park since 1994.

GLENNA LUSCHEI is the editor of *Solo Press* and has been publishing it for 35 years. She was Poet Laureate for San Luis Obispo city and county for the year 2000. She is currently working on her PhD in Hispanic Languages at the University of California, Santa Barbara.

SARAH MACLAY's recent poems appear in *Ploughshares, Field,* and *Hotel Amerika.* Her first full-length book, *Whore* (2003 Tampa Press Poetry Prize), is just out from UT Press. Her reviews and essays appear in *Poetry International, The Writer's Chronicle* and *Poetix.*

AMY MACLENNAN has work published in *Rattle, South Dakota Review, Gingko Tree Review, Wisconsin Review, Convergence, SLANT* and *Confluence.* One of her poems was included in *So Luminous theWildflowers,* and she received a first place award in the 2003 Ina Coolbrith Circle poetry contest.

MELANIE MARTIN was born and raised in California. She has traded in sirens for crickets by moving to Southern Illinois where she is earning her MFA in poetry in Carbondale and was an assistant editor for *Crab Orchard Review*.

HOLADAY MASON lives and works in the California Venice. Her work has appeared in numerous publications, including *Poetry International*, *Spoon River Review*, *Comstock review* and *Cider Press Review*.

ELLYN MAYBE is the author of two full-length collections of poetry, *The Cowardice of Amnesia* and *Walking Barefoot in the Glassblowers Museum*. She has given readings both nationally and internationally. She currently studies film in Prague.

MICHAEL MCCLINTOCK resides in South Pasadena and Fresno, California. His short poems have been widely anthologized, including in *The Haiku Anthology*, ed. by Cor van den Heuval (W. W. Norton, 1999).

DANIEL MCGINN has hosted the weekly reading at Beans Coffee House, been a regular contributor to Next Magazine and the O.C. Weekly and represented Los Angeles at the National Poetry Slams. He is the author of several chapbooks and his poems have appeared in many publications, most recently in *Political Affairs*, *November 3rd Club*, *The Blue Mouse* and *Spillway*.

LORI MCGINN has been playing scrabble with the same man for 27 years. She is the author of *Waiting* by Inevitable Press. Her favorite days are rainy, cookie baking days.

JOSHUA MCKINNEY is the author of two award-winning books of poetry: *Saunter* (University of Georgia Press, 2002) and *The Novice Mourner* (Bear Star Press, 2005). He is an Associate Professor of English at California State University, Sacramento.

MICHAEL B. MCMAHON teaches at Fresno Pacific University, a small school in the San Joaquin Valley. His poems have appeared in such magazines as *Seneca Review*. *Green Mountains Review*, *Notre Dame Review*, and *Atlanta Review*. His translations of Jesus Serra's book of poems *Páramos en la Memoria*, has been reissued by the University of Andes Press.

JUNE MELBY received the City of Hamburg, Germany, Kulturbehorde artist award and residency in 2003. She grew up on a miniature golf course in Wisconsin.

BILL MOHR lived in California between 1960 and 2004, when he received a Ph.D. from the University of California, San Diego, and moved east to teach at St. John's University and Rutgers University. He will return to the Los Angeles area in June, 2006, and has no desire to live elsewhere ever again. His latest collection of poems, *Bittersweet Kaleidoscope*, is forthcoming from If Publications.

CAROL MOLDAW grew up in the Bay Area, and is the author of three books of poetry: *The Lightning Field*, winner of the 2002 FIELD Poetry Prize, *Chalkmarks on Stone*, and *Taken from the River*, as well as a chapbook, *Through the Window*. She lives in New Mexico.

JIM NATAL is the author of two poetry collections, *Talking Back to the Rocks* (Archer Books, 2003) and *In the Bee Trees* (Archer Books, 2000), which was a finalist for the Pen Center West and Publishers Marketing Association Awards.

KRISTY NIELSEN has published work in *Mid-American Review*, *The Madison Review*, *Cimarron Review*, *Kalliope*, and *Spoon River Poetry Review*, among others. She was born in Detroit and has lived in California for ten years.

KIM NORIEGA is a Southern California poet whose work has appeared in the *Maggee Park Poets' Anthology* and International Living's *Parler-Paris Newsletter* on-line and in March of 2003 she participated in the UNESCO "Dialogue Through Poetry" reading in Paris. She has taught poetry workshops to elementary age children and is currently working on a poetry program for women recovering from alcoholism and eating disorders. She lives in San Diego with her husband, Ernie.

JAMIE O'HALLORAN was born on Long Island, raised there, New Orleans and Seattle. Her poems have appeared in magazines such as *Solo, The Cream City Review* and *Yankee*, and in anthologies, including the premiere *So Luminous the Wildflowers: An Anthology of California Poets*, and *And What Rough Beast: Poems at the End of the Century*. She lives in Los Angeles where she teaches 8th grade English.

MAUREEN ELLEN O'LEARY is a writer who lives in Oakland, California. She is a member of the English Faculty at Diablo Valley College where she teaches writing and literature.

JUDITH S. OFFER has four books of poetry, and has been published in about fifty magazines, large and small. Her best-known venue was on the National Public Radio program All Things Considered. She is also a playwright, with fourteen produced plays.

DAVID OLIVEIRA is the author of *In the Presence of Snakes* (Brandenberg Press, Santa Cruz). He is co-editor of *How Much Earth: The Fresno Poets* (Heyday Books, Berkeley). He is the Poet Laureate of Santa Barbara and lives in Phnom Penh, Cambodia.

JUDITH PACHT is an author and poet whose work has been published in journals such as *Gastronomica*, University of California Press. *SOLO 6* and *Site of the City*, a postcard competition. Her poems appear in several poetry collections and the 2002 anthology, *So Luminous the Wildflowers*.

JAIMES PALACIO has been published throughout the U.S., Japan and England. Among his accomplishments he is most proud of his appearances in several prestigous literary antholigies, including twice in *Art Life*, and two previous Tebot Bach anthologies. Currently he is working on a comic novel involving, among others, Amelia Earheart and a six-foot Sasquatch named Steve.

SHERMAN PEARL co-edits CQ (California Quarterly) and was a co-founder of the Los Angeles Poetry Festival. His work is widely published and has won several national and international awards (including the 2002 National Writer's Union competition).

CANDACE PEARSON manages to live the life of a recluse in a big noisy city. From her airy garret up 62 steps in the Los Angeles hills, she has written two poetry collections about farms and rivers and is working on a collection about memory.

SAM PEREIRA's third book, *A Café in Boca*, is due to be published by Tebot Bach in 2006. He teaches English in the San Joaquin Valley of California, where he lives a quietly substantial life, with his wife, the writer, Susan R.G. Pereira.

ROBERT PETERS' thirtieth volume of poetry *Makars' Dozens,* fresh from Pearl Edition is now out now. His greatest joys presently are casino hopping, crosswords, and Scrabble.

CAROL POTTER is the author of three books of poetry, the most recent *Short History of Pets* which won the Cleveland State University Poetry Center Award and the Balcones Award. She won a Pushcart Prize in 2001 and has recent publications in *Field* and *The Iowa Review.*

PADMA RUBIALES RAJAOUI's poetry has been published or is forthcoming in the *Bay Area Poets Coalition's Anthology, Bellowing Ark, Byline, Connecticut River Review, Caveat Lector* and *Chiron Review.*

AARON J. ROBERTS lives in Mission Viejo, CA with his wife Lisa and their two cats Eliot and Emily. He has been writing for several years and has had featured readings throughout Southern California. He is the author of three chapbooks entitled: *Reinventing Taon, My Aardvark Is Worse Than My Bite,* and *Laundry Day.* Previous publication credits include *ARTLIFE* and *Spillway.*

ROBERT RODEN received his M.F.A. from CSULB in June of 2001, then promptly moved to northern California to join the new gold rush near Sacramento. He teaches at American River College and Sierra College, and co-edits *The Silt Reader,* a pocket poetry magazine.

ZACK ROGOW's fifth book of poems, *Greatest Hits: 1979–2001,* was published by Pudding House Publications. He edited a new anthology of U.S. poetry, The Face of Poetry, published by University of California Press in 2005. He is the editor and artistic director of *TWO LINES: A Journal of Translation* and teaches in the MFA in Writing Program at the California College of the Arts.

DANNY ROMERO was born and raised in South Los Angeles. He is the author of the novel *Calle10* (1996) and two chapbooks of poetry *P/V* (1997) and *Land of a Thousand Barrios* (2002). He teaches in the English Department at Sacramento City College.

LEE ROSSI is the author of the recently published *Ghost Diary,* as well as an earlier collection, *Beyond Rescue.* His poems have appeared in numerous anthologies and journals including the *Sun, Poetry East, Nimrod,* and the *Southern Indiana Review.*

C. J. SAGE is the editor of *The National Poetry Review* and the producer of Cupertino public radio's weekly poetry program. Her poems have appeared in *The Threepenny Review, Smartish Pace, Ginko Tree Review,* and numerous other magazines and anthologies.

MEHNAZ SAHIBZADA was born in Pakistan and raised in California. She is currently working toward her Ph.D. in Religious Studies at UC Santa Barbara. She writes poetry and fiction and is the process of writing on a novel entitled Curry and Cacti.

DIXIE SALAZAR is a visual artist, poet and novelist who lives in Fresno, California. Her first collection of poetry, *Reincarnation of the Commonplace,* won the National Poetry Contest and was published by Salmon Run Press in 1998. Her newest collection of poetry, *Blood Mysteries,* was published by University of Arizona Press in 2002.

CATHIE SANDSTROM SMITH's work has appeared in *Solo*, *Lyric Poetry Review*, *So Luminous the Wildflowers*, *Cider Press Review*, *Matchbook*, and Poetry in the Windows III and V.

ANNE SILVER had been a poet since 1968. Her current book is *Bare Root: A Poet's Journey through Breast Cancer*. Anne was an international expert witness in handwriting issues in Chinese, Hebrew, Farsi and English. She passed away in October, 2005.

JOAN JOBE SMITH, founding editor of *Pearl* and *Bukowski Review* has published many books of poetry, notably *Jehovah Jukebox*, about her 7 years as a go-go girl in Southern California during early 1970s and *Pow Wow Cafe* (Smith Doorstop), finalist for the 1999 UK Forward Prize.

BARRY SPACKS teaches at UC Santa Barbara. The most extensive of his seven volumes of poetry is *SPACKS STREET: NEW AND SELECTED POEMS* from Johns Hopkins. He has a CD out, "A Private Reading," presenting 42 selected poems from 50 years of work.

MIKE SPRAKE has been living in this country for a quarter of a century, and the American dream is still one. Every morning he wakes up hoping to be transformed into something better, but he still has to pull on his work boots and make a living, like most other poets he knows.

DAVID STARKEY is the author of a textbook, *Poetry Writing: Theme and Variations* (NTC, 1999), several collections of poetry, and more than 300 poems published in literary journals around the world. He was born in Sacramento and currently lives in Santa Barbara.

JEREMY STEPHENS is a student at Fullerton College. He's been the featured reader at the *Two Idiots Peddling Poetry* series in Orange County, as well as part of group features during the 2002 OC Poetry Festival, and WorldFest 2003.

JUDITH TAYLOR is the author of *Selected Dreams from the Animal Kingdom* and *Curios*. Her work has appeared in *American Poetry Review*, *Antioch Review*, *Fence*, *Pleiades*, *Field*, and *Volt*. The recipient of a Pushcart Prize, she resides in Los Angeles and co-edits POOL.

SUSAN TERRIS' poetry books include *Natural Defenses*, *Fire Is Favorable To The Dreamer*, and *Poetic License*. With CB Follett, she is co-editor of an annual anthology, *Runes, A Review Of Poetry*. Her next book *Contrariwise* will be published by Time Being Books in 2007.

LYNNE THOMPSON is a native of Los Angeles whose work has appeared or is forthcoming in *The Indiana Review*, *Runes*, *Louisiana Literature*, *Rattle*, *Yabolusha Review*, *Solo* and *Pearl* as well as the online 'zines *Samsara Wuarterly*, *Moondance* and *Mentress Moon*.

CARINE TOPAL lives and works in the South Bay. Her poems have appeared in *The Best of the Prose Poem*, *Caliban*, *Pacific Review*, and many others. She is a recipient of the Jane Kenyon Poetry Prize from Water-Stone. Her first collection of poems is entitled *God As Thief*.

BEN TRIGG lives in Anaheim, CA. He is co-host of Two Idiots Peddling Poetry at the Ugly Mug Caffe in Orange. Chapbooks include: *Fragments and Without Fear*. Recent publication credits include: *Incidental Buildings and Accidental Beauty* and *So Luminous the Wildflowers*.

DUANE TUCKER is an actor and a writer. He has over 75 Film and TV credits. He has been widely published and had several screenplays optioned. He is currently performing his one-man show on John Muir in Canada.

KATHLEEN TYLER's poetry has appeared or is forthcoming in numerous journals including *Runes, Solo*, *Margie*, *Coe Review*, *Visions International* and *Poetry Motel*. Her first book of poetry, *The Secret Box*, will be published in June, 2006 by Mayapple Press.

AMY UYEMATSU is a third generation Angelino and Japanese-American. Her third collection of poems, *Stone Bow Prayer* was published in 2005 by Copper Canyon Press. Her previous books are *Nights of Fire, Nights of Rain* and *30 Miles from J-Town* (both from Story Line Press).

After dropping out of Ph.D. school in English literature, FRED VOSS has spent 30 years finding poetry in the hearts and souls of the men and women working in America's factories, steel mills and machine shops.

CHARLES HARPER WEBB's latest book of poems, *Tulip Farms and Leper Colonies*, was published in 2001 by BOA Editions, Ltd. In 2002, the University of Iowa Press published *Stand Up Poetry: An Expanded Anthology*, edited by Webb. Recipient of grants from the Whiting and Guggenheim foundations, he teaches at California State University, Long Beach.

FLORENCE WEINBERGER is the author of two published collections of poetry, *The Invisible Telling Its Shape* (Fithian Press, 1997) and *Breathing Like a Jew* (Chicory

Blue Press, 1997), and a manuscript, *Carnal Fragrance*, to be published by Red Hen Press.

JAN WESLEY teaches at the college level after a quarter of a century in the film business, and received her MFA from Vermont College, where she was a Ruth Lily Award nominee. Her poems have appeared in *Spillway*, *Runes*, *Solo*, *Rattle*, *Saturday Afternoon Journal*, *Yalobusha Review* and *The Comstock Review* (Special Merit & Finalist for the Muriel Craft Bailey Award).

LEIGH WHITE is an award winning advertising copywriter, graphic designer and illustrator who has been writing poetry since 1998. Her chapbook, *Dropped As A Baby* was published by farstarfire Press in 2002.

KATHERINE WILLIAMS has two chap books with Inevitable Press, *Lapsed Existentialist* (1998), and *Shadowplay* (1999). The Sunland/Tujunga Public Library Poetry Series sponsored her in the 2001 LA Poetry Festival Curators' Choice Gala.

JOY WILSON is a California Native currently living in Oxford, MS at Ole Miss where she teaches creative writing. She recently graduated from the MFA program there.

CECILIA WOLOCH is the author of *Sacrifice* and *Tsigan: The Gypsy Poem*, both from Cahuenga Press, and *Late*, recently published by BOA Editions, Ltd. She is the director of Summer Poetry in Idyllwild and a member of the faculty of the MFA Program in Poetry at New England College. Widely traveled, she currently maintains residences in Los Angeles and Atlanta.

GAIL WRONSKY is the author of *Poems for Infidels* (Red Hen Press), *Dying for Beauty* (Copper Canyon Press), and other books. Her poems and reviews have appeared in many journals and anthologies. She is Director of Creative Writing and Syntext at Loyola Marymount University in Los Angeles and lives in Topanga Canyon.

ROBERT WYNNE holds an MFA in Poetry from Antioch University and is the co-founder and co-editor of Cider Press Review, an annual poetry journal. He has won the Academy of American Poets College Award and the Poetry Super Highway Online Poetry Contest. He is the author of 4 chapbooks, most recently *What the Body Knows* (2002, Pudding House Press), and his work has appeared in numerous magazines including *Solo*, *Poetry International*, *Two Rivers* Review and *Rattle*.

BRENDA YATES works and lives in Los Angeles with her husband. Recently, her work has appeared *in Cider Press Review*, *So Luminous the Wildflowers* and *Pearl*.

KIM YOUNG is a writer for a non-profit organization in Los Angeles. She is a graduate student at California State University Northridge and has been awarded the Academy of American Poetry Prize, the Benjamin Saltman Poetry Award and the Rachel Sherwood Poetry Prize.

RICH YURMAN has been writing for more than 45 years. His work has appeared in numerous literary magazines. His most recent chapbooks are *GIRAFFE*, March Street Press (2002), and *FASCINATION DOLLS*, Snark Publishing (2003).

acknowledgements

NEIL AITKEN: 'After Neruda' from *Beyond the Valley of Contemporary Poets 2004 Anthology* © by Neil Aitken and used by permission of the author.

NEIL AITKEN: 'Pomello' © by Neil Aitken and used by permission of the author.

WILLIAM ARCHILA: 'This is for Oscar' from *The North American Review* © by William Archila and used by permission of the author.

CAROL W. BACHOFNER: 'History' © by Carol W. Bachofner and used by permission of the author.

JOAN E. BAUER: 'On The Poetics of the Text' from *The Comstock Review* © by Joan E. Bauer and used by permission of the author.

RICHARD BEBAN: 'Heroes' © by Richard Beban and used by permission of the author.

MARJORIE BECKER: 'Furrows in the Open Land' © by Marjorie Becker and used by permission of the author.

LORY BEDIKIAN: 'Night in Lebanon' from *Crab Orchard Review*, Volume 8, Number 1, Fall/Winter, 2002 © by Lory Bedikian and used by permission of the author.

KEVEN BELLOWS: 'Losing It' from *Taking Your Own Time* © by Keven Bellows and used by permission of the author.

LAUREL ANN BOGEN: 'Safety Pin' from *Washing a Language*, Red Hen Press, 2004 © by Laurel Ann Bogen and used by permission of the author.

LAUREL ANN BOGEN: 'Sanctuary' from *Place as Purpose: Poetry from the Western States*, Autry Museum of Western Heritage/Sun & Moon Press, 2002 © by Laurel Ann Bogen and used by permission of the author.

DEBORAH EDLER BROWN: 'Still Lives' © by Deborah Edler Brown and used by permission of the author.

DERRICK BROWN: 'A Short Song' from *I'm Easier Said Than Done*, Tank Farm, 2003 © by Derrick Brown and used by permission of the author.

LINDA BROWN: 'Coyote Darshan' from *Journey With Beast: Poems 1970-2004*. La Jolla Poets Press, © 2004. © by Linda Brown and used by permission of the author.

MARK C. BRUCE: 'Elegy for a Goldfish' © by Mark C. Bruce and used by permission of the author.

CHRISTOPHER BUCKLEY: 'Dispatch from Santa Barbara, 2001' from *Rivendell* © by Christopher Buckley and used by permission of the author.

ELENA KARINA BYRNE: 'Paradise Mask' © by Elena Karina Byrne and used by permission of the author.

MARY CAHILL: 'A Letter For V' © by Mary Cahill and used by permission of the author.

R.G. CANTALUPO: 'Almost Flying' from *The Wisconsin Review* © by R.G. Cantalupo and used by permission of the author.

JOHN CASEY: 'Barbie and Ken In the Garden of Eden' from *Cobalt Café Broadside Series* © by John Casey and used by permission of the author.

CARLOTA CAULFIELD: 'Tres Cuentos Chinos' from *Movimientos metalicos para juguetes abandonados, Spain: Consejeria de Cultura of Canary Islands, 2003* © by Carlota Caulfield and used by permission of the author.

JEANETTE CLOUGH: 'The Day's Space' © by Jeanette Clough and used by permission of the author.

MARCIA COHEE: 'April Quartet' from Barnes & Noble Poetry Contest © by Marcia Cohee and used by permission of the author.

WANDA COLEMAN: 'Daddyboy' from *Imagoes*, Black Sparrow Press, 1983 © by Wanda Coleman and used by permission of the author.

LARRY COLKER: 'Classified Ads, May 1, 1608' from *Poetry in the Windows V* © by Larry Colker and used by permission of the author.

BRENDAN CONSTANTINE: 'Last Night I Went to the Map of the World and I Have Messages for You' from *Beyond the Valley of the Contemporary Poets Anthology* © by Brendan Constantine and used by permission of the author.